why trilling matters

yale

university

press

new haven

and

london

adam

kirsch

why

trilling

matters

"Why X Matters" and the yX logo are registered trademarks of Yale University.

Yale University Press books may be purchased in quantity for educational, business, or promotional use. For information, please e-mail sales.press@yale.edu (U.S. office) or sales@yaleup.co.uk (U.K. office).

Set in Adobe Garamond type by Keystone Typesetting, Inc., Orwigsburg, Pennsylvania. Printed in the United States of America.

Library of Congress Cataloging-in-Publication Data
Kirsch, Adam, 1976–
Why Trilling matters / Adam Kirsch.
   p. cm. — (Why X matters)
Includes bibliographical references and index.
ISBN 978-0-300-15269-2 (alk. paper)
1. Trilling, Lionel, 1905–1975—Criticism and interpretation.
2. Criticism—United States—History—20th century. I. Title.
PS3539.R56Z84 2011
818'.5209—dc22
2011014923

A catalogue record for this book is available from the British Library.

This paper meets the requirements of ANSI/NISO Z39.48-1992 (Permanence of Paper).

10 9 8 7 6 5 4 3 2 1

books by adam kirsch

Benjamin Disraeli
The Modern Element: Essays on Contemporary Poetry
Invasions: Poems
The Wounded Surgeon: Confession and
    Transformation in Six American Poets
The Thousand Wells: Poems

To Jonathan Rosen

contents

I does literature matter?

"We are all a little sour on the idea of the literary life these days. . . . In America it has always been very difficult to believe that this life really exists at all or that it is worth living." To anyone who has been paying attention to the morale of American writers lately, such a diagnosis will come as no surprise. Hardly a year goes by without a novelist, poet, or critic coming forward to confess this sense of sourness, which is actually a compound of despair and resentment. Despair, because every department of literature seems to be undergoing simultaneous crisis, a multiple organ failure of the kind that inevitably leads to death; resentment, because of the contemporary American writer's sense that he has been like the final investor in a Ponzi scheme, having bought into the venerable enterprise of literature only to discover that it is on the verge of default.

Poetry, of course, was the first to go. Already in 1991, in his essay "Can Poetry Matter?" Dana Gioia declared that "American poetry belongs to a subculture. No longer part of the mainstream of artistic and intellectual life, it has become the specialized occupation of a relatively small and isolated group." As a poet, Gioia looked covetously at the attention and esteem given to fiction: "A reader familiar with the novels of Joyce Carol Oates, John Updike, or John Barth may not even recognize the names of Gwendolyn Brooks, Gary Snyder, or W. D. Snodgrass." But five years later, Jonathan Franzen lamented in his essay "Perchance to Dream" that whatever attention the novel continued to receive was just "consolation for no longer mattering to the culture." The poet might envy the novelist, but the novelist has his own jealousies: "there are very few American milieus today in which having read the latest work of Joyce Carol Oates or Richard Ford is more valuable, as social currency, than having caught the latest John Travolta movie or knowing how to navigate the Web."

In the last few years, technological change and economic recession have combined to accelerate this long-term crisis.

First local bookstores disappeared, victims of the chain stores and Amazon: since the 1990s, more than half of America's independent bookstores have closed. The newspaper book review was next: in the 2000s, the *Los Angeles Times, Washington Post,* and many other major papers shrank or eliminated their book sections. Cynthia Ozick, in her 2007 essay "Literary Entrails," performed the same kind of obsequies for literary criticism that Gioia and Franzen had done for poetry and fiction: "What is missing is an undercurrent, or call it, rather (because so much rests on it), an infrastructure, of serious criticism."

University English departments are suffering: as long ago as 1999, in an essay titled "The Decline and Fall of Literature," Andrew Delbanco observed that "Literature is a field whose constituency and resources are shrinking." Even as it lost students to more pragmatic disciplines, English was also losing its intellectual identity: "it has become routine to find notices in the department advertising lectures on such topics as the evolution of Batman . . . alongside posters for a Shakespeare conference." Reading itself, according to a 2004 study by the National Endowment for the Arts, is in "dramatic decline, with fewer than half of American adults now reading literature . . . [and] the steepest rate of decline . . . occurring in the youngest age groups."

For many readers and writers, all these anxieties find their ultimate focus in a fear that the book itself, the site and symbol of literature for the last five hundred years, is about to disappear, replaced by the Kindle or iPad or something equally suspect. Margaret Atwood expressed the fears of many readers over the age of, say, thirty when she wrote, "This is crucial, the fact that a book is a thing, physically there, durable, indefinitely reusable, an object of value . . . electrons are as evanescent as thoughts. History depends on the written word."

At such a moment, how could we not be "a little sour on the idea of the literary life," or find it hard "to believe that this life really exists at all"? It may be surprising to learn that this complaint was made in 1952, just at the midcentury moment to which Franzen and Ozick look back so enviously. But the greater surprise is that it was Lionel Trilling who made it. For in the last twenty years, when writers have lamented the decay of literature's confidence and authority, they have often turned, as if by instinct, to Trilling as the emblem of those lost virtues. More than any twentieth-century American intellectual, Trilling stood for the principle that society and politics cannot be fully understood without the literary imagination. In his own career, he combined the traditional authority of the academic—he was a professor of English at Columbia for four decades—with the new authority of the freelance intellectual—some of his most important essays were written for "little magazines" like *Partisan Review.* His best-known book, the essay collection *The Liberal Imagination* (1950), continues to define an epoch in

American intellectual history. When he died in 1975, at the age of seventy, the critic Steven Marcus paid tribute to his "spiritual heroism" on the front page of the *New York Times*.

It is so hard, today, to imagine this kind of honor being paid to a literary critic—perhaps to any writer—that Trilling's name is often invoked as a reproach to the fallen present. According to Delbanco, the cure for the decline and fall of literature is a return to Trilling's ideal of literary education, as set forth in his essay "The Uncertain Future of the Humanistic Educational Ideal": an "exigent experience," in which "an initiate . . . became worthy of admission into the company of those who are thought to have transcended the mental darkness and inertia in which they were previously immersed." Ozick contrasts Franzen's longing for a mass audience with Trilling's recommendation, in "The Function of the Little Magazine," that a writer "direct his words to his spiritual ancestors, or to posterity, or even, if need be, to a coterie." This is what she describes as Trilling's "self-denying purity; purity for the sake of a higher purity."

Yet how can this help sounding like a little too much purity —like what Milton, in the *Areopagitica*, calls "an excremental whiteness"? "Assuredly we bring not innocence into the world, we bring impurity much rather; that which purifies us is trial, and trial is by what is contrary," the poet writes, and there has always been a tendency, among Trilling's critics, to rebel against an elevation which they construe as mere abstemiousness. "He never gives the impression of having read anything for the first time, of being surprised, confused, delighted, enraged, or captivated by anything he has read," Roger Sale complained in 1973. Stefan Collini, writing thirty-five years later, catches the same tone: "There is, for many of us, something vaguely oppressive about the thought of having to reread Lionel Trilling now. We can't help feeling that we should be improved by Trilling, and this feeling is itself inevitably oppressive. . . . Reading him keeps us up to the mark, but we can't help but be aware that the mark is set rather higher than we are used to."

In all these descriptions, whether their intention is laudatory or the opposite, it is clear that Trilling is being assigned the role of literature's superego. As a student of Freud, Trilling himself would have known what must follow: for if the superego is the savage enforcer of unattainable cultural ideals, then the ego's health and happiness require that the superego be humbled. This need simultaneously to honor and humble Trilling is responsible for the curious ambivalence with which he is usually written about today. In the last ten years, much of Trilling's work has been brought back into print: *The Moral Obligation to Be Intelligent,* the generous selection of essays edited by Leon Wieseltier; the new editions of *The Liberal Imagination* and *The Middle of the Journey,* from New York Review Books; even the manuscript of his unfinished novel, published as *The Journey*

Abandoned. And each of these publications has been greeted with considerable attention, in the form of reviews by leading critics—even if those reviews are largely defensive and skeptical in tone. Trilling is, apparently, still close enough, still authoritative enough, to need to be reckoned with, which sometimes means rejected and mocked.

There could be no more Oedipal gesture than Louis Menand's, when he marked the publication of a new edition of *The Liberal Imagination* by suggesting that Trilling was basically a pathetic figure. "He was depressive, he had writer's block, and he drank too much," Menand wrote in *The New Yorker* in 2008. "He did not even like his first name. He wished that he had been called John or Jack." All this is meant to cut Trilling down to size, preparatory to cutting his work down to size:

> But the idea that people have some sort of moral obligation to match up their taste in art and literature with their political opinions exercised a much more powerful appeal in Trilling's time than it does today. . . . Since the 1960s, cultural taste has largely been liberated from politics. . . . educated people tend to be culturally promiscuous and permissive. They don't use the language of approval and disapproval in their aesthetic responses; they simply like some experiences and dislike other experiences.

During the culture wars of the 1970s and 1980s, Trilling was often attacked from the right and the left for being insufficiently adaptable to their respective purposes. There was a nice symmetry to this abuse: Cornel West condemned Trilling as the "Godfather of Neo-Conservatism," while Norman Podhoretz complained that "almost always he fought against being called a conservative." But such attacks at least implied that Trilling's allegiances mattered, that he was a writer whose legacy had to be claimed or disclaimed. To critics like Menand, on the other hand, Trilling is simply out of date, and like everything obsolete in our present-minded culture, he carries a faint odor of the absurd. Why did Trilling *worry* so much about these things? Why couldn't he "simply like some experiences and dislike other experiences," in the passionless, unassuming way of the consumer who prefers one brand to another?

On the one hand, a literary culture suffering from a crisis of weightlessness, a feeling that literature has ceased to matter in the way it did for Trilling and his age; on the other, a critical consensus that regards Trilling as a suffocating ghost, because he believed that literature mattered too much. These mixed feelings are both a sign of how much Trilling continues to matter today—critics like Irving Howe or Alfred Kazin, once Trilling's peers in the circle of New York intellectuals, do not provoke the same kind of confused passion—and a symptom of how his achievement has been misunderstood.

In making my own arguments for why Trilling matters, I hope that I can benefit from what might seem like a disadvantage. Unlike the critics I've quoted, I have no memory of Trilling personally, or even of a literary culture in which he was a figure of authority. On the contrary, when I was an undergraduate English major in the mid-1990s, I don't believe Trilling was ever assigned or discussed in any of my courses. I first came to him on my own, and though I found people to encourage my enthusiasm, I always read Trilling for pleasure, not from obligation.

Part of the pleasure, certainly, came from the authority of Trilling's judgments, and of the prose which conveys those judgments. But Trilling's authority, like all genuine literary authority, is itself a literary achievement—not a privilege of cultural office or a domineering assertion of erudition and intellect, but an expression of sensibility, the record of an individual mind engaged with the world and with texts. This is true of all the best literary critics, but it seems especially true of Trilling, who is surprisingly uninterested in the traditional prerogatives and responsibilities of criticism. In his major essays, collected in *The Liberal Imagination, The Opposing Self,* and *Beyond Culture,* he does not bring news of important new writers or teach us how to read difficult new works, the way Edmund Wilson does. Nor does he offer a polemical revaluation of literary history, the way F. R. Leavis does. Nor, finally, does he try to push contemporary literature in the direction of his own ambitions, the way poet-critics like T. S. Eliot and Allen Tate were doing so influentially in his lifetime.

If Trilling's essays are not exactly literary criticism, it is because they are something more primary and more autonomous: they belong to literature itself. Like poems, they dramatize the writer's inner experience; like novels, they offer a subjective account of the writer's social and psychological environment. And like all literary works, Trilling's essays are ends in themselves—they are autotelic, to use a word that Eliot coined to describe what criticism could never be. This helps to explain why there has never been a Trilling school of criticism. He does not offer the reader findings or formulas, which might be assembled into a theory; he offers what literature alone offers, an experience.

This is, of course, an experience of a more restricted and abstract kind than the poet or the novelist can give. The drama of Trilling's essays comes from the reaction of a powerfully individual sensibility, not to emotions or human situations or the world as a whole, but to certain texts and ideas. This means it occurs at two removes from life, and can never have the immediacy or breadth of appeal that creative writing has. But it is a genuine drama, because Trilling was the rare kind of writer for whom an idea is itself an experience. He may have been exaggerating when he wrote that "Ideas and moral essences are, to all people, the most interesting things in the world"; but if they aren't that to all people, they certainly were to Trilling himself.

This helps to explain two of the most important, and sometimes controversial, aspects of Trilling's style. One is his cultivation of a short list of key words, which return again and again in his essays, to the point that they seem to bear his trademark: moral, liberal, will, mind, reality. These are large and general words, and so they are natural targets for skepticism. To Collini, Trilling's "Big Words make us a little uncomfortable nowadays, and we have difficulty using them other than in a knowing, allusive way."

It is true that Trilling's key words are momentous, and that he does not fear momentousness. But it is also crucial not to ignore the deliberately tentative and exploratory way he uses them. "Moral" and "liberal," in particular, recur in Trilling's work like themes in a piece of music or symbols in a poem: rather than becoming simpler with repetition, they accumulate dimensions and implications. "Liberal" means one thing to Trilling when writing about Matthew Arnold and E. M. Forster in the 1930s and early 1940s, and something very different, almost contradictory, when he praises "the liberal imagination" in the late 1940s. Trilling had an almost poetic interest in the unfolding of these master terms, which strike such a deep chord in his imagination.

The other feature of Trilling's prose, which readers have noticed and sometimes resisted from the very beginning, is his use of the first person plural—the famous Trilling "we." His essay

"Reality in America," from *The Liberal Imagination,* offers a characteristic example:

> We live, understandably enough, with the sense of urgency; our clock, like Baudelaire's, has had the hands removed and bears the legend, "it is later than you think." But with us it is always a little too late for mind, yet never too late for honest stupidity; always a little too late for understanding, never too late for righteous, bewildered wrath; always too late for thought, never too late for naïve moralizing.

Who, one might reasonably ask, is included in this "us"? In the preface to his 1965 book *Beyond Culture,* Trilling mentioned the objection of a reviewer who "said that when I spoke of what 'we' think or feel it was often confusing because sometimes it meant 'just the people of our time as a whole; more often still Americans in general; most often of all a very narrow class, consisting of New York intellectuals as judged by [my] own brighter students at Columbia.'" Trilling genially acknowledged that "this may well be an all too accurate description of my practice."

But at least readers who encountered Trilling's essays in the pages of *Partisan Review,* or were in the audience hearing him deliver a paper (some of his most important essays started out as lectures), could feel that they were undoubtedly being addressed by him—that they belonged to Trilling's "we." Today, the device can feel coercive: isn't Trilling demanding that the reader subscribe to a cultural diagnosis which, in fact, she may want to contest? (What if I *don't* feel that my clock has had its hands removed?) Worse, it can seem to exclude: if Trilling in this passage is chastising left-liberals of the 1940s, isn't he speaking about a local, long-vanished cultural pathology, which is now of merely historical interest?

Here, again, Trilling's language must be understood in its literary intention. Poems and novels benefit from familiar conventions that make it easy for the reader to enter into the writer's experience. The lyric "I" is not as autobiographical, nor the omniscient narrator as impartial, as they appear: each is really an invitation disguised as a proposition, and their authority is not asserted but justified (if it is justified) by the insight and pleasure that they make possible. In a similar way, Trilling, in dramatizing his own experience of a book or a writer, is offering himself up as the reader's surrogate. To enroll in Trilling's "we" is to enter into his experience, not to submit slavishly to his judgments; the commonality it expresses is provisional and literary, not sociological. Properly understood, it is a humbler form of address than if Trilling were to write "I," which would turn him into an authority handing down judgments, or to write in the third person without addressing the reader at all. His "we" is an improvised, and sometimes clumsy, attempt to make his writing about texts as involving as other people's writing about characters and plots.

It is an ironic sign of the success of this strategy that today, in our unmistakably fragmented literary culture, Trilling looks like an icon of centrality and authority—to be yearned for or despised, depending on your inclination. Ozick, who is one of Trilling's truest critical successors, yearns for it: she writes longingly of the days "when Lionel Trilling prevailed at Columbia, [and] Edmund Wilson, Irving Howe, and Alfred Kazin enlivened the magazines, decade upon decade." All of these writers were associated, at one time or another, with *Partisan Review.* Yet when Trilling wrote "The Function of the Little Magazine," his introduction to a tenth-anniversary anthology of writing from *Partisan Review,* he began by noting the irony that it was considered "a notable achievement" if a magazine devoted "to the publication of good writing of various kinds" is able to attract an audience of six thousand readers. If this was a "victory," Trilling wrote wryly, it took place in "the larger circumstance of defeat."

This is not to say, of course, that good writing never reaches a substantial audience. When *The Liberal Imagination* was published in 1950, it sold 70,000 copies in hardcover and 100,000 in paperback, numbers that might well induce an envious nostalgia. Yet consider the case of Jonathan Franzen, who in 1996 complained about the "deafening silence of irrelevance" that greeted his first two novels, despite their warm reviews. In 2001, he went on to sell millions of copies of *The Corrections,* which came as close to "mattering to the culture" as any novel of the last twenty years. Yet in 2002, Franzen published an essay about the novelist William Gaddis that began by discussing the angry letters he got about *The Corrections* from readers who found the book difficult and elitist. He felt guilty, he wrote, about violating the implied "contract" between writer and reader, since "the deepest purpose of reading and writing fiction is to sustain a sense of connectedness."

Why is it that Trilling, with his six thousand readers, felt that he had established a sense of connection with his proper audience, while Franzen, with his millions of readers, worried about the vastly greater number of people he couldn't reach? The answer must be that things like relevance, connection, and "mattering," while absolutely central to a writer's sense of success and failure, cannot be measured quantitatively. Franzen, realizing how insignificant the biggest bestseller is compared to the audience for a movie or a videogame, is haunted even in success by "the larger circumstance of defeat." Trilling, half a century earlier, faced exactly the same realization: "After all, the emotional space of the human mind is large but not infinite, and perhaps it will be pre-empted by the substitutes for literature—the radio, the movies, and certain magazines." But he refused the emotional blackmail exerted in America on "the writer who does not write for 'the many.'"

It is in this context that Trilling makes the statement Ozick alludes to in "Literary Entrails": "The writer must define his audience by its abilities, by its perfections, so far as he is gifted to conceive them. He does well, if he cannot see his right audience within immediate reach of his voice, to direct his words to his spiritual ancestors, or to posterity, or even, if need be, to a coterie. The writer serves his daemon and his subject." But is this really, as Ozick says, "self-denying purity; purity for the sake of a higher purity?" To read it that way would be to mistake the force of Trilling's own ambition, and his sympathy with the ambition of the great novelists. "Of all practitioners of literature," he writes in "Art and Fortune," "novelists as a class have made the most aggressive assault upon the world, the most personal demand upon it, and no matter how obediently they have listened to their daemons they have kept an ear cocked at the crowd and have denounced its dullness in not responding with gifts of power and fame."

Trilling, then, is far from denying the kind of ambition that makes Franzen long openly for big sales and cultural power. What he recognizes, however, is that these longings are never satisfied in a straightforward way, at least for modern writers. In a review of Joyce's letters, Trilling writes that "On the evidence that [*Ulysses*] provides, there is nothing that can signalize the artist's achievement of success in life. There is no person, let alone a social agency, competent and empowered to judge his work and tell him that he has triumphed with it, that he has imposed his will upon the world and is now to be feared and loved." And this is *Ulysses*, universally considered the greatest English-language novel of the twentieth century. To triumph like Joyce, it seems, is not to win power, celebrity, and riches, but to win fame—which means, the enduring devotion of the best readers, and perhaps the sense of having pleased the divine reader whom Milton called "all-judging Jove."

When a writer dreams of wealth and power, he is always half-conscious that these things exist for him mainly as metaphors. To live the literary life, as a writer or as a reader, is to live ideally—which means, often, to live in despite of reality, or better, to insist on the reality of what most people regard as merely ideal. This is one reason why Trilling is so alert to another trap that continues to waylay American writers: the idea that fiction ought to justify itself by paying homage to reality, conceived as brute sociological fact. Trilling was not at all opposed to realism, on theoretical or ideological grounds, the way later postmodernist critics would be. On the contrary, in "Manners, Morals, and the Novel," he made a classic defense of the nineteenth-century realist novel's fascination with money and status: "Every situation in Dostoevsky, no matter how spiritual, starts with a point of social pride and a certain number of rubles," he observes.

Tom Wolfe invoked Trilling when he called for a return to realism, in his 1989 manifesto "Stalking the Billion-Footed

Beast": "Lionel Trilling was right when he said . . . that what produced great characters in the nineteenth-century European novel was the portrayal of 'class traits modified by personality.' " But when Wolfe goes on to contrast his own brand of virile, masculine, democratic realism with an effete, intellectual, socially disengaged postmodernism, he falls into exactly the error that Trilling himself warned against. On one side, Wolfe writes, there are avant-garde writers like John Hawkes, John Barth, and Robert Coover, "brilliant . . . virtuosos," who write "clever and amusing" fiction within "narrow limits"; on the other, there is Wolfe himself, who embraces "the American century," who has a strong enough digestion to handle the "feast spread out before every writer in America." This is exactly the same kind of tendentious, middle-brow binarism that Trilling condemned in "Reality in America," and the summary he gives in that essay of the thought of V. L. Parrington, a once-influential literary historian, fits Wolfe to a T:

> There exists, he believes, a thing called *reality*; it is one and immutable, it is wholly external, it is irreducible. Men's minds may waver, but reality is always reliable, always the same, always easily to be known. And the artist's relation to reality he conceives as a simple one. Reality being fixed and given, the artist has but to let it pass through him, he is the lens in the first diagram of an elementary book on optics. . . . Sometimes the artist spoils this ideal relation by "turning away from" reality. This results in certain fantastic works, unreal and ultimately useless.

The problem with a sociological or journalistic definition of realism, Trilling perceives, is the implication that the mind and the imagination are not part of reality. As he complains in "Manners, Morals, and the Novel," "reality, as conceived by us, is whatever is external and hard, gross, unpleasant," whereas "whenever we detect evidence of style and thought we suspect that reality is being a little betrayed." *Reality Hunger,* the recent manifesto by the novelist David Shields, is far more sophisticated than Wolfe's, but even Shields demonstrates something of this same impatience with fiction as invention: "Cut to the chase. Don't waste time. Get to the real thing," he writes.

The supreme prestige of reality in America—"the word 'reality' is an honorific word," Trilling observes—is what makes it so "very difficult to believe" that the "literary life really exists at all" here. That is because, in a sense, it does not "really" exist; it exists, but otherwise. By the same token, the current crisis of confidence in bookselling, publishing, journalism, and so on, can make it much more difficult to be a writer or a reader; but it cannot finally lead to the death of literature, because literature does not live by those things in the first place. Trilling preserved a healthy suspicion of what he considered the American prejudice in favor of the concrete and countable, the tendency to see quantity as a more real measurement than quality. The Kinsey Report, he wrote, was typically American in its "extravagant fear of all ideas that do not seem . . . to be, as it were, immediately dictated by simple physical fact." Because the Report's "principles of evidence are entirely quantitative," a matter of counting orgasms and sexual partners, it could never go "beyond the conclusion that the more the merrier." And if this is not a satisfactory way of measuring sexual contentment, how much less suited is it to talking about literary achievement?

"Generally speaking," Trilling wrote, "literature has always been carried on within small limits and under great difficulties." What sustains writers and readers under those difficulties is, above all, the consciousness of one another's existence. This is, in fact, the consolation that Franzen finds at the end of "Perchance to Dream": "in a suburban age, when the rising waters of economic culture have made each reader and each writer an island, it may be that we need to be more active in assuring ourselves that a community still exists." But the name of the activity by which readers and writers communicate—by which they make the private experience of reading into the common enterprise of literature—is criticism. "The fact is," Trilling writes, "that an actual response to art (in our culture at least) depends on discourse—not upon any one kind of discourse, but upon discourse of *some* kind." That is why Gioia longs for poetry critics like the ones who flourished in the mid-twentieth century, who "charged modern poetry with cultural importance and made it the focal point of their intellectual discourse"; and why Ozick dreams of a "superior criticism

[that] not only unifies and interprets a literary culture but has the power to imagine it into being."

Even Trilling, who embodied the kind of critical authority that Ozick and Gioia find us in need of, himself felt a need for the reassurance and community that only criticism can provide. His remarks about feeling sour on the literary life come in a short essay on Edmund Wilson, in which he remembers how Wilson's example sustained him during the Great Depression: "for me, and for a good many of my friends, Wilson made [the literary life] a reality and a very attractive one. He was, of course, not the only good writer of the time, but he seemed to represent the life of letters in an especially cogent way, by reason of the orderliness of his mind and the bold lucidity of his prose . . . and because of the catholicity of interests and the naturalness with which he dealt with the past as well as with the present."

The very terms in which Trilling praises Wilson suggest how different they are as critics. Wilson, with his confident rationalism, his cosmopolitan scope, and what Trilling calls his "old-fashioned, undoctrinaire voracity for print," was a perfect representative of literature as a profession. Trilling, who wrote much less than Wilson and imparted a greater sense of ambivalence to what he did write, represents literature as a way of life. In the chapters that follow, I explore how Trilling's most intimate ambitions and concerns—above all, his sense of the conflict between the artist's will and the demands of justice—shape and are shaped by the different phases of his reading, writing, and teaching. By considering Trilling not just as a cultural or political figure, but as an interpreter of his own experience, I hope to emphasize the part of his achievement that has meant most to me: his demonstration of what it means to create one's self through and against the books one reads. At a time when the possibility of reading in this existentially engaged way seems to be in doubt—a development that Trilling himself foresaw—no critic could be more inspiring, or more necessary.

2
"a professor and a man and a writer"

Perhaps the biggest obstacle to a genuine appreciation of Trilling today is a certain interpretation of his life and work that has been growing in popularity for years, and has now become a kind of critical orthodoxy. This is the notion that Trilling was, at heart, not a great literary critic but a failed novelist, and therefore an unhappy, unsatisfied man. Once this view is accepted—and it can be found in most of the important discussions of Trilling in recent years, even the sympathetic ones—it's hard to escape the conclusion that we don't have to admire or learn from Trilling, only pity him.

The seeds of this idea were planted in 1984, when his widow Diana Trilling, herself a noted critic and intellectual, published excerpts from his journals in *Partisan Review*. Because Trilling's public demeanor had been so impressively dignified and reserved, it came as a shock to read his private expressions of dissatisfaction with his life and work, verging at moments on self-contempt. In particular, it seemed, Trilling never stopped regretting that he had not managed to become a novelist, publishing just one full-length work of fiction, *The Middle of the Journey*, and a handful of short stories. In 1961, when Ernest Hemingway died, Trilling wrote: "Except Lawrence's 32 years ago, no writer's death has moved me as much—who would suppose how much he has haunted me? How much he existed in my mind—as a reproach? He was the only writer of our time I envied." These private reflections helped to fill in an autobiographical picture Trilling had merely sketched in a lecture in 1971:

> I am always surprised when I hear myself referred to as a critic. . . . If I ask myself why this is so, the answer would seem to be that in some sense I did not ever undertake to be a critic—being a critic was not, in Wordsworth's phrase, part of the plan that pleased my boyish thought, or my adolescent thought, or even my thought as a young man. The plan that did please my thought was certainly literary, but what it envisaged was the career of a novelist. To this intention, criticism, when eventually I began to practice it, was always secondary, an afterthought: in short, not a vocation but an avocation.

When Trilling said this, he was speaking as the most famous and authoritative literary critic in the English-speaking world. He could hardly have suspected that decades later, some readers would take his words as meaning that he considered himself a failure. Here, for instance, is how Geraldine Murphy begins her introduction to *The Journey Abandoned,* her edition of Trilling's second, unfinished novel: "Lionel Trilling is best known today as a literary critic, but he thought of himself as a writer, a novelist foremost. Just as Milton considered prose the work of his left hand, so Trilling regarded his own critical writing." Menand agrees that "Lionel Trilling was not completely happy about being Lionel Trilling."

As is usually the case with posthumous revelations, however, the news about Trilling's self-dissatisfaction, and his powerfully mixed feelings toward novels and novelists, can only be news to those who have not read his work carefully. His failure is, in any case, relative: *The Middle of the Journey,* published in 1947, is still in print more than sixty years later, and it remains both a compelling story and an important document of the intellectual climate of the 1930s. But it is true that the novel did not live up to Trilling's highest ambitions, and that he was disappointed in its reception—especially by Robert Warshow's negative review in *Commentary,* which argued that "Trilling, lacking an aesthetically effective relationship to experience, is forced to translate experience into ideas, embodying these ideas in his characters and giving his plot the form of an intellectual discussion reinforced by events."

This is just the problem one might expect in a novel written by a critic, and it is certainly true that *The Middle of the Journey* usually treats its characters as representatives of ideas rather than as free creations. In Arthur and Nancy Croom, Trilling portrays the "advanced," fellow-travelling leftism of the mid-1930s, with its combination of guilt and privilege; in Gifford Maxim, the memorable character based directly on former Soviet spy Whittaker Chambers, Trilling portrays the ex-Communist who has turned into a religious reactionary, without ever losing his ideological absolutism. These forces do battle for the soul of John Laskell, the literary, liberal figure who is the novel's closest thing to a surrogate for Trilling himself. Trilling even uses Laskell to voice his own fears that he will have to forsake his creative ambitions: "Now and then Laskell remembered with a kind of regret he had once dreamed of fame, even of immortality, where now he was concerned only with a sound professional reputation. But his willing sacrifice of his young ambitions—which, after all, could never have been fulfilled—made the work he had chosen all the more valuable to him."

But if it is true that the characters in *The Middle of the Journey* are spokesmen for ideas, it is not fair to say, as Warshow did, that this is due to Trilling's lack of an "aesthetically effective relationship to experience." Rather, what becomes clear in reading the novel is that the elements of experience that Trilling cared about most were, precisely, ideas. The human drama that interested him was the drama of individuals shaping their ideals and morals in reaction to texts.

It is striking, in fact, how many of the key episodes in the book concern reading, and how Trilling uses characters' responses to texts in order to illuminate their psychology. To Nancy Croom, Oswald Spengler's *Decline of the West,* with its vision of inexorable historical cycles, is unacceptable on political grounds: it is "entirely reactionary because it cut off all hope of the future." To her neighbor Emily Caldwell, the book teaches a different lesson: "to live your life, to snatch the moment, because the cycles just keep on and on, and in the end what does anyone ever have except perhaps a little fleeting moment of happiness?" Laskell knows that Nancy's reaction is the enlightened and correct one, and feels embarrassed for Emily, who is so naïve she doesn't realize that Spengler is behind the times—that "for this book a vocabulary of discussion had existed a few years ago and had then died." Yet Trilling also makes clear that Emily's reaction has its own truth, that she is able to draw an existential lesson from Spengler that Nancy is too narrow and fearful to hear.

The different ways these two characters read a text foreshadow the ways they will react to major events in the plot, including Laskell's dangerous illness and the climactic death of Emily's young daughter Susan. Indeed, that deliberately melodramatic ending (Trilling once wrote of "my very strong feeling . . . that a novel must have all the primitive elements of story and even of plot—suspense, surprise, open drama and even melodrama") is triggered by another difference of literary interpretation, having to do with the proper way to recite William Blake's poem "Jerusalem." Susan, declaiming the poem at a small-town talent show, stamps her foot childishly to accent the line "I will not cease from Mental Fight"—a gaucherie that Laskell had previously warned her against. Realizing that she has made a mistake, Susan freezes, and Laskell prompts her with the next line; whereupon her father Duck, incensed at the way Laskell has usurped his paternal role, comes out of the audience and strikes Susan down.

This is pretty far-fetched, and reading *The Middle of the Journey,* it is hard to avoid the sense that it is the literary and intellectual confrontations that really matter to Trilling, while the confrontations between characters are extensions or illustrations of them. That is exactly why Trilling's decision, after the novel was published, to turn finally from fiction to criticism was such a fruitful one. The critical essay, as Trilling wrote it, was the right genre to dramatize the collision of ideas; his essays distill the essence of his fiction, and allow him to give greater scope to the true workings of his mind than the novel or short story could. Having written his first book on Matthew Arnold, he doubtless remembered the justification Arnold offered for turning from poetry to criticism: "But is it true that criticism is really, in itself, a baneful and injurious employment; is it true that all time given to writing critiques on the works of others would be much better employed if it were given to original composition, of whatever kind this may be? Is it true that Samuel Johnson had better have gone on producing more *Irenes* instead of writing his *Lives of the Poets?*"

Just so, three years after publishing *The Middle of the Journey,* a good novel, Trilling brought out *The Liberal Imagination,* a great work of criticism. And it would be a serious mistake to think that he didn't know it—that his regret over failing to be a novelist, voiced ironically in public and bitterly in the privacy of his diary, superseded his knowledge of what he accomplished as a critic. The cliché of the critic as thwarted creator—the eunuch in the harem—is so familiar, and so useful to readers who dislike the feeling of being "kept up to the mark" by Trilling, that it is frequently used in defiance of Trilling's express judgment.

Thus Murphy, like several other recent writers on Trilling, quotes the following sentences from his notebook, written in 1948 after he was promoted to full professor at Columbia: "Suppose I were to dare to believe that one could be a professor and a man! and a writer!—what arrogance and defiance of convention." Even Ozick reads these lines as a confession of failure, remarking: "Here was bitterness, here was regret: he did not believe that a professor could be truly a man; only the writer, with his ultimate commitment to the wilderness of the imagination, was truly a man."

But here is how the notebook entry, as published in *Partisan Review,* actually reads: "But sometimes I feel that I pay for the position not with learning but with my talent—that I draw off from my own work what should remain with it. Yet this is really only a conventional notion, picked up from my downtown friends, used to denigrate myself & my position, to placate the friends, to placate in my mind such people as Mark V[an] D[oren], who yearly seems to me to grow weaker & weaker, more academic, less a person. Suppose I were to dare to believe that one could be a professor and a man! and a writer!—what arrogance and defiance of convention. Yet deeply I dare to believe that—and must learn to believe it on the surface." In other words, Trilling's confession of failure is exactly the reverse: it is a declaration of confidence, and a rejection of the "conventional notion" that selective quotation seems to ascribe to him. The fear that a professor and critic could not be a man and a writer was only "on the surface"; "deeply," in his conscience, he knew that he was both, that criticism was the form that best suited his literary imagination.

This is not to deny that Trilling's inability to write great fiction was significant. Born in 1905, he came of age at a time when the modern novel was experiencing its greatest triumphs: Proust, Joyce, Mann, and Lawrence were all producing their masterpieces just at the time Trilling was starting to think of himself as a writer. (When he was 22, he even reviewed the English translation of Proust's *Cities of the Plain*, one of his first published pieces.) "Being a novelist," Lawrence had written, "I consider myself superior to the saint, the scientist, the philosopher, and the poet," and Trilling almost instinctively conceded this superiority. In his unfinished novel, Harold Outram—like John Laskell a failed novelist—ruefully expresses what the novel meant to writers who started out in the 1920s:

> Ah yes—your generation no longer worships the novel. In my time it was novel or nothing. We spent our days getting ready for it, looking for experience. An *honest* novel it had to be—honest was the big word. And always one novel was what we thought of. Only one, very big, enormous. Then, having laid this enormous egg, I suppose we expected to die. It had to be big and explosively honest—you'd think we were collecting dynamite grain by grain, you'd think we were constructing a bomb. We expected to blow everything to bits with our honesty.

Outram's is not meant to be a trustworthy voice—having failed at literature, he has become a Communist ideologue, and he goes on to say that "Russia has perceived before any of us that the arts, about which we are so politically sentimental, are one of the great barriers in the way of human freedom and decency." But his self-satire does seem to reflect Trilling's own ironic perspective on his early novelistic ambitions.

Unlike Outram, however, Trilling's discouragement did not lead him to turn vengefully against literature itself. On the contrary, Trilling's disappointment as a novelist was the most productive experience in his literary life. To use a metaphor he mistrusted, it was the wound to his bow. For in thinking about why he could not write like the novelists he admired, Trilling was brought up against the gulf between aesthetic ideals and ethical ideals, between the energies of art and the disciplines of civilization, that would be his master subject. Only a writer who had lived this division, who allowed it to shape his destiny, could have written about it as movingly and insightfully as Trilling does. "It is one of the necessities of successful modern story," Trilling wrote apropos of Henry James, "that the author shall have somewhere entrusted his personal fantasy to the tale." In this sense, above all, his own criticism is literary in inspiration.

Trilling's notebook entries show that he returned to this question—the price of art, and whether it was worth paying—throughout his life, in the most personal terms. As early as 1927, when he was just twenty-one, he worries about a character in a story he is writing: "Unfortunately (because, I suppose, it will be a 'self-portrait') he cannot be very interesting: that is, he will have no real physical or emotional abnormality. Perhaps it might be well to give him one soon, but I fear he will always be the least dramatic person in the book, no matter what he does, because the most intellectual—i.e. he will be seeing most." To be "interesting" and "dramatic," he already believes or intuits, means being less than fully self-aware. Only people who are prevented by some mental or social handicap from "seeing," from full self-consciousness, can have the kind of force that a novelistic character—or a novelist—must bring to bear. And he himself, he already knows, is too gifted or cursed with consciousness to have that kind of instinctive power.

This idea becomes ever more explicit in the notebooks. In 1933, Trilling writes about seeing a letter that Hemingway had written while drunk: "a crazy letter . . . self-revealing, arrogant, scared, trivial, absurd: yet felt from reading it how right such a man is compared to the 'good minds' of my university life— how he will produce and mean something to the world . . . how his life which he could expose without dignity and which is anarchic and 'childish' is a better life than anyone I know could live, and right for his job. And how far-far-far I am going from being a writer. . . ." Sixteen years later, he has a similar reaction to the young Jack Kerouac: "not wanting K's book to be good because if the book of an accessory to murder is good, how can one of mine be? The continuing sense that wickedness—or is it my notion of courage—is essential for creation." As late as 1967, some twenty years after he last published any fiction,

Trilling feels the same way about the Jewish American novelists then in vogue:

> Whether or not the artist derives his powers from neurosis, he certainly derives them from a species of insanity, from megalomania, from his absurd belief in his own myth. This is what accounts for the achievement of Mailer and Bellow and even Malamud. They believe they are great men, they insist on being the center of their universe: all revolves around them. To impose, to impose: this is their single aim; it acts as a real thing, although it arises out of the absurdity. I defeated myself long ago when I rejected the way of chutzpah and mishagass in favor of reason and diffidence.

It is not true, of course, that all creative writers live lives as "crazy," "wicked," and "absurd" as Hemingway, Kerouac, or Mailer—as Trilling knew full well. If he singled them out as examples of the kind of writer he could never be, it was because they exemplified the problem into which he had special insight: that modern literature stands in an adversarial relationship to modern civilization, that the works of great writers, even more than their lives, challenge the very principles by which their readers live. "It seems to me that the characteristic element of modern literature," Trilling wrote, "or at least of the most highly developed modern literature, is the bitter line of hostility to civilization which runs through it."

Trilling is the dramaturge of this conflict, setting the part of himself that shares this hostility against the part that fears and resists it. By admitting both sides of this dialectic into his writing, he becomes a proxy for the reader, inviting "us" to reflect on the experience of division that we, in our encounter with modern literature and life, cannot escape. In this way, Trilling became the kind of writer that he praised in "Reality in America":

> A culture is not a flow, nor even a confluence; the form of its existence is struggle, or at least debate—it is nothing if not a dialectic. And in any culture there are likely to be certain artists who contain a large part of the dialectic within themselves, their meaning and power lying in their contradictions; they contain within themselves, it may be said, the very essence of the culture, and the sign of this is that they do not submit to serve the ends of any one ideological group or tendency.

3 varieties of liberal imagination

"A writer's reputation often reaches a point in its career where what he actually said is falsified even when he is correctly quoted," Trilling observed in the preface to his first book, *Matthew Arnold.* "It is very easy for Arnold's subtle critical dialectic to be misrepresented and for his work to be reduced to a number of pious and ridiculous phrases about 'the grand style,' 'culture,' 'sweetness and light.'" It seems fitting, then, that Trilling, who modeled his career on Arnold's in certain ways and found in him a kindred spirit, should have his own reputation follow the same course and reach the same point. He, too, is commonly reduced to a few famous phrases, most of which come from one book— *The Liberal Imagination*—and especially from that book's preface. It is here that Trilling writes that "in the United States at this time, liberalism is not only the dominant but even the sole intellectual tradition"; and describes his own mission as "putting under some degree of pressure the liberal ideas and assumptions of the present time"; and urges that liberals must learn from literature the "essential imagination of variousness and possibility, which implies the awareness of complexity and difficulty."

If the goal of a preface is to give readers a simple, catching summary of a complex work, to make a book seem immediately relevant, then the preface to *The Liberal Imagination* has succeeded only too well. It allows readers to believe that Trilling was primarily a critic of the political illusions of the American left in the postwar period. The preface is dated December 1949, just months before the start of the Korean War, which makes it even more tempting to read the book as a symptom of America's retreat from New Deal liberalism, into a more guarded and self-critical Cold War liberalism. One of the best recent studies of Trilling, *The Conservative Turn* by Michael Kimmage, pairs him with Whittaker Chambers—who, unlike Trilling, belongs to the history of politics, rather than literature—and interprets his literary values in immediately political terms. "An art that was morally complex and free from self-righteousness," Kimmage writes, "would express the spirit of political anti-communism." Similarly, on the back cover of the most recent edition of *The Liberal Imagination,* the reader is informed that it appeared during "one of the chillier moments of the cold war," and in the introduction that "the first thing to say about *The Liberal Imagination* is that it is a cold war book."

This way of looking at Trilling, as an ideologist of liberal anti-Communism, is of course not wrong. He was involved in the soul-searching debates among the erstwhile radicals of the *Partisan Review* circle, and he was convinced that liberal indulgence of Stalinism was a political and cultural disaster. But to read *The Liberal Imagination* simply as a document of its time is to underestimate Trilling's literary achievement, and implicitly to deny that it still matters today. There are no more fellow-travellers in American intellectual life—there is nothing left to fellow-travel with. Liberals in the age of Obama face plenty of challenges, and even some temptations, but they are not the same ones that liberals faced in the age of Truman. If *The Liberal Imagination* is still a living work, then—and the excitement it can still produce in readers proves that it is—it must be more than a Cold War book.

One way to gauge the breadth and complexity of Trilling's purpose, in fact, is to notice the ways in which he designed the book to resist a parochial political reading. To take *The Liberal*

Imagination as a guide to politics or political philosophy—to seek in Trilling's liberalism for the liberalism of Roosevelt and Truman, or of Locke and Mill—is a recipe for frustration. By far the most misleading sentence in the "Preface" is the one in which Trilling deplores the liberal tendency to trust too much in "delegation, and agencies, and bureaus, and technicians": this amounts to a red herring, since liberalism in the sense of an activist state is virtually absent from the book. The word liberal, as Trilling uses it, is deliberately elusive: what it names is at once an emotional tendency, a literary value, an intellectual tradition, and a way of being in the world. Only sometimes, and as it were incidentally, does Trilling speak of liberalism as a position in American politics.

This happens most directly, perhaps, in one of the least famous essays in the book, "Kipling," where Trilling laments the swaggering imperialism of Rudyard Kipling's work—not for itself, but because it presents liberals with such an easy target for moral condescension. "Kipling was one of liberalism's major intellectual misfortunes," Trilling writes, because "he tempted liberals to be content with easy victories of right feeling and with moral self-congratulation." So easy was it to despise Kipling's cult of manliness and militarism that, Trilling recalls, his own generation came to despise courage itself as reactionary: "I remember that in my own undergraduate days we used specifically to exclude physical courage from among the virtues." This recollection gives Trilling's "us," in this context, an especially local and personal feel: when he writes that "for many of us our rejection of [Kipling] was our first literary-political decision," he is counting on readers of his generation and background to agree.

In this way, "Kipling" carries out the program of the Preface pretty exactly: it criticizes a liberal shibboleth from within the liberal ranks. In both the Preface and "Kipling," Trilling alludes to the same passage from John Stuart Mill's essay on Coleridge, in which the liberal philosopher praised the conservative poet and "said that we should pray to have enemies who make us worthy of ourselves." Since his own generation has no such respectable conservative voice to learn from, only unfashionable reactionaries like Kipling, it is up to a liberal like himself to insist on the wisdom hiding behind Kipling's bluster.

Trilling notices, for instance, the way "Kipling's sympathy was always with the administrator and he is always suspicious of the legislator." Trilling does not exactly endorse this view—he calls it "foolish, but . . . not the most reprehensible error in the world"—but he senses in it a lesson the statist liberal might well learn, having to do with the difference between framing a benevolent law and effectively carrying it out. A better conservative than Kipling "might make clear to the man of principled theory, to the liberal, what the difficulties not merely of government but of *governing* really are." It is not so far from this empiricist skepticism to the impulse that led some New York intellectuals, in the 1960s, to critique the welfare state in Irving Kristol's magazine *The Public Interest.* At such moments, the intellectual genealogy that connects Trilling with neoconservatism becomes visible.

In the same years that he was writing the essays collected in *The Liberal Imagination,* Trilling published a number of pieces in the vein of "Kipling": explicitly polemical and political essays, in which he rebuked liberal conventional wisdom. In particular, and in keeping with the anti-Stalinist climate of opinion at *Partisan Review,* he criticized the cultural tendency associated with the Popular Front—that is, the willingness of American liberals to follow the Communist Party line in politics and culture. Yet it is striking that these essays, which hew so closely to the program Trilling lays out in the Preface, were the ones he chose *not* to include in *The Liberal Imagination.*

One of Trilling's best summaries of the Popular Front mindset, as it informs American literature, comes in an essay published in *Partisan Review* in 1938, "The America of John Dos Passos." Among the main beliefs of this "cultural tradition," he writes, are that "the fate of the individual is determined by social forces; that the social forces now dominant are evil; that there is a conflict between the dominant social forces and other, better, rising forces; that it is certain or very likely that the rising forces will overcome the now dominant ones." In other words, the conventional Depression-era liberal accepts the Marxist view that history is driven by class conflict, and looks forward to a Marxist revolution in the United States. It is this emphasis on the collective and the progressive, Trilling argues, that makes Popular Front liberalism deleterious to literature, especially the novel, which is necessarily subversive of collective values and primarily interested in the individual. "Too insistent a cry against the importance of the individual quality is a sick cry," Trilling writes, and warns that "it is not at all certain that it is political wisdom to ignore what so much concerns the novelist."

Here, if anywhere in Trilling's work, is the "essential imagination of variousness and possibility," used to critique *bien-pensant* simplemindedness. The same technique can be found in an essay of 1940 on "T. S. Eliot's Politics," in which Trilling once again quotes Mill on Coleridge, urging liberals to learn from the conservative Eliot that "man cannot be comprehended in a formula," that human nature is too flawed to permit of "any such ultimate moral victory as will permit the 'withering away of the state.'" He almost hits on the very language he will use in the Preface a decade later, describing "the sense of complication and possibility, of surprise, intensification, variety, unfoldment, worth," whose "more or less abstract expressions we recognize in the arts."

In a note on this essay, which was collected after Trilling's death in *Speaking of Literature and Society,* Diana Trilling writes that he apparently considered including it in *The Liberal Imagination,* but decided against it. No reason is given; but aside from any literary reservations he may have had about the Eliot essay, or the one on Dos Passos, it seems likely that what led Trilling to exclude them is precisely their overwhelming pertinence to contemporary culture and politics. That is, Trilling did not want the book to read like a polemic against the Popular Front, or an intervention in a debate among Cold War liberal intellectuals. Instead, he designed the book in such a way that immediate issues are only the point of entry, the local habitation, of a more permanent debate—which is, as always in Trilling, preeminently a debate with himself.

The Liberal Imagination is, in fact, the culmination and resolution of a crisis of conscience that occupied the first two decades of Trilling's life as a writer. The origins of this crisis are hard to trace in the book itself, though they would have been understood implicitly by many of its first readers, since Trilling's experience was the common one of his literary generation. As a teenager and young adult during the 1920s, he came of age in a climate of triumphant modernism, when American culture was undergoing a liberating renaissance. Then, just as he entered adulthood, the crash of 1929 and the subsequent Depression brought this period to a terrifying halt. The mood among writers became harshly self-critical: What had the modernist experiment really been worth, if it left readers blind to imminent social catastrophe?

Even worse, for liberals, was the fact that so many of the modernist masters appeared to side with the forces of reaction, which were triumphant in Europe. As Trilling was to observe time and again, "Yeats and Eliot, Proust and Joyce, Lawrence and Gide—these men do not seem to confirm us in the social and political ideals which we hold." Was it not the writer's duty, at a moment of crisis, to join in the struggle for a better society, for the revolution—and to use his talent as a weapon in the struggle? In 1932, Edmund Wilson led a group of prominent writers (including John Dos Passos and Sherwood Anderson) in circulating a "Manifesto" that proclaimed: "in our function as writers, we declare ourselves supporters of the social-economic revolution—such revolution being an immediate step toward the creation in the United States of a new human culture based on common material possession, which shall release the energies of man to spiritual and intellectual endeavor."

This same urgency erupts in Trilling's early writing with shocking suddenness. As late as 1930, in a review of a book called "Portrait of the Artist as an American," he could insist that, even "as the social and moral problems of the modern world become more insistent," purely literary standards of judgment must be upheld: "criticism can be valid only if it thinks in terms of the individual work and its accomplishment or failure . . . and not in terms of social causes." Yet in the same year, writing about three novels of gritty, low-life realism, Trilling speaks with a very different voice—engaged, radical, ferociously political, in a way that must surprise any reader who knows only the grave and balanced style of the mature critic.

"We are living," Trilling writes, "in an environment that is befouling and insulting." In the atmosphere of the Depression, it is impossible to write affirmatively about American society: "there is only one way to accept America and that is in hate; one must be close to one's land, passionately close in some way or other, and the only way to be close to America is to hate it." This hate allows the novelist to see through the surface of American culture and perceive that "at the bottom of America there is insanity." And the best novels are those which, like Edward Dahlberg's *Bottom Dogs* and Nathan Asch's *Pay Day*, plunge the reader deepest into this insanity. For the reader who protests that this approach is not truly literary but sociological —a reader, perhaps, like the Trilling who once refused to judge art "in terms of social causes"—this new Trilling has only contempt: "The implication behind the 'sociological' sneer is that this sort of book is not 'literature,' and it illustrates admirably the blindness of 'literary' critics. Realism is perhaps never productive of great art. But America must, by the conditions of its life, be committed to realism for a long time yet, for painful contact with environment will not soon cease, and we cannot in literature avoid the bases of our life."

It is ominous to find Trilling, of all people, putting the word literature in scare quotes—as though literature were a bourgeois conspiracy to hide the truth about capitalist society. Yet even in this essay, which represents Trilling at his most radical, it is noteworthy that he cannot quite bring himself to commit the ultimate sin against literature, which is to hold that politically effective writing equals good writing. He continues to distinguish between "realism"—by which he means, here, naturalistic protest fiction—and "great art," even though he insists, rather penitentially, that the America of 1930 doesn't deserve the latter.

This scruple never quite disappears, even as Trilling devotes himself, in the early 1930s, to the cause of the revolution. Reviewing *The Nineteen,* a propaganda novel by the Soviet writer Aleksandr Fadeyev—who would later become Stalin's chief literary enforcer—he praises it for depicting "a set of ethical and emotional values so fine that, if revolution be necessary to secure them, revolution becomes desirable." But even so, Trilling can't stop himself from writing, "so touching and so pure are the deeds and the motives in this novel that one almost distrusts it."

In a 1930 essay on D. H. Lawrence, Trilling endorses the novelist's hatred of "the sensitive middle class," writing, "the proletariat may be crippled in body; it is not further diseased by the parasite of mind." Most telling of all, perhaps, in 1933

Trilling reviews a book of Coleridge's letters, and for the first time quotes Mill's praise of Coleridge, which would become such a touchstone for him—but he quotes it in a spirit of blackest irony, in the course of arguing that Coleridge was a fascist, "the chief transmitter" of the philosophy "which fascism, both in Italy and Germany, is now using to rationalize its fight against socialism." The poet he would later honor as the wisest of conservatives he now holds responsible for Hitler and Mussolini.

In this brief, explosive period, Trilling offers a perfect negative of what would become his life's work. In his mid-twenties, he despises the middle class, denigrates mind, and dismisses the autonomy of literature; for the rest of his career, and especially in *The Liberal Imagination,* he would write to educate the middle class, insist on the cultivation of mind, and defend the autonomy of literature. It is not hard to see that some spirit of repentance was at work, a feeling of guilt for the force and suddenness with which he had sacrificed his true self on the altar of politics. In "Art and Fortune," one of the most personal essays in *The Liberal Imagination,* Trilling writes, "To live the life of ideology with its special form of unconsciousness is to expose oneself to the risk of becoming an agent of what Kant called 'the Radical Evil,' which is 'man's inclination to corrupt the imperatives of morality so that they become a screen for the expression of self-love.'" It may seem overdramatic to say that

Trilling ever participated in radical evil; but it is plain that his writing of the early 1930s was what allowed him to understand the perils of ideology from the inside. When he refers to his fellow liberals as "we," it is because he has shared their temptations, and tried to liberate himself from them.

The attempt to mediate the claims of literature and politics would be the deep purpose of Trilling's work over the next two decades. This becomes explicit in *The Liberal Imagination,* but it is equally true of the two books he produced before it: *Matthew Arnold,* a critical biography published in 1939, and *E. M. Forster,* a short study he wrote "in a concentrated rush" in 1943. The similarities between these two subjects are striking, and suggest how, throughout his career, Trilling would be drawn to writers whom he could use as mirrors or metaphors for his own experiences. Both Arnold and Forster, after all, were liberal critics of liberalism—writers who wanted to undermine the pieties of the intellectual class to which they belonged. Both tried to vindicate literature as a social good, while preserving its imaginative independence from utilitarian pressures.

For Trilling, still struggling with his novelistic ambitions, there was also a certain significance in the fact that both Arnold and Forster were writers who stopped writing creatively. Arnold turned from poetry to criticism, while Forster didn't write another novel after *A Passage to India,* in 1924, though he lived until 1970. What Trilling says about Arnold, in the first pages of his book, reads in retrospect like a veiled confession: "He perceived in himself the poetic power, but knew that his genius was not of the greatest, that the poetic force was not irresistible in him, that it might not be able to carry before it all else in his personality. He knew he had the right power to make poetry but that it lacked something of assertiveness, that it was only delicately rooted in him." This tentativeness is surely related to the quality that Trilling, many years later, remembered drawing him to Arnold in the first place, his melancholy: "All I knew about Matthew Arnold I had derived from an affection for some of his poems whose melancholy spoke to me in an especially personal way. I thought it would be interesting to discover and explain in historical-cultural terms why he was so sad."

The movement in that last sentence, from personal emotion to "historical-cultural" causes, is very characteristic of Trilling. He would not have denied, of course, that the reasons why writers are sad, or joyful, or anything else, are private and biographical, as much as they are public and historical; or that the effect of a literary work has as much to do with its aesthetic and rhetorical strategies as with its cultural context. But he resisted making either psychology or rhetoric the focus of his criticism, in part because, during his lifetime, both of these approaches were highly influential, with what he saw as lamentable results. The former led to Freudianizing psychobiography, what Trilling described in "Freud and Literature" as "the method which finds the solution to the 'mystery' of such a play as *Hamlet* in the temperament of Shakespeare himself and then illuminates the mystery of Shakespeare's temperament by means of the solved mystery of the play." To focus on linguistic technique, on the other hand, was the approach of the New Critics, who insisted on studying every poem as a self-contained object, a "well-wrought urn." The problem here, Trilling wrote in "The Meaning of a Literary Idea," is that "critics who are zealous in the defense of the autonomy of art . . . presume ideas to be only the product of formal systems of philosophy, not remembering . . . that poets too have their effect in the world of thought."

What Trilling objects to, in each case, is a critical doctrine that leaves no place for the will of the artist. To see a literary work as an expression of trauma and neurosis, or as a poised structure of ambiguities, is to forget that writers write for a conscious purpose—in fact, a double purpose: to propagate certain ideas about nature, society, and man, and to assert the writer's own claim to power and honor. "My inclination," Trilling writes in "On the Teaching of Modern Literature," is "to pay attention chiefly to what the poet *wants*." His own desire to become a novelist may not have allowed Trilling to write great fiction, but it gave him first-hand experience of what many critics do not understand: the tremendous will of the artist, and the moral dubiousness of that will.

It is here, in Trilling's intimate knowledge and suspicion of the artistic will, that the origins of his political quandary can be found. In the turmoil of the early 1930s, the imperative of social justice seemed to make all merely personal ambitions contemptible; only art that served the common good could be permitted at such a time. Yet Trilling could not long silence his knowledge that great art, of the kind he had grown up admiring and wanting to create, was not the product of humanitarian concern, but of a private will that is, if not exactly selfish, at least inseparable from personal hopes and desires. Already by 1934, he was recovering his sense that it is the superbness and superiority of the artist, not his serviceableness, that matter: "If it is the essential fact about a hundred proletarian novels that they show the misery of the working class, their growing consciousness, their militant struggle and finally their victory, there are then ninety-nine novels too many," he wrote in a review.

If art is understood to be fundamentally at odds with justice, however, then the falling silent of writers like Arnold and Forster cannot be regarded simply as a misfortune. It could be that the growth of conscience inevitably leads the writer away from literature, as Arnold seems to suggest in a passage Trilling quotes:

> Whoever seriously occupies himself with literature will soon perceive its vital connection with other agencies. Suppose a man to be ever so much convinced that literature is, as indisputably it is, a

powerful agency for benefiting the world and for civilizing it, such a man cannot but see that there are many obstacles preventing what is salutary in literature from gaining general admission, and from producing due effect. Undoubtedly, literature can of itself do something towards removing these obstacles and towards making straight its own way. But it cannot do all.

Arnold's metamorphosis from poet to literary critic, and then to social critic, can thus be seen as a tale not of genius snuffed out, but of imagination tamed and made useful by conscience. Speaking of Arnold's criticism, Trilling writes, "Its keynote is activism and affirmation . . . Arnold sees now that he must move beyond individual psychology to what so largely determines the quality of the mind itself—to society." This is one potential solution to the bad conscience of literature, from which Trilling was suffering in the very years he was writing the doctoral dissertation that would become *Matthew Arnold*. (Indeed, he would recollect that the writing of such a book at such a time sometimes struck him as absurdly irrelevant: "it seemed to me that I was working in a lost world, that nobody wanted, or could possibly want, a book about Matthew Arnold.")

In E. M. Forster, Trilling finds a different strategy for subduing the fierce ambition of the artist. It is true that Forster, like Arnold, gave up imaginative writing at a surprisingly early stage in his career. But even in his fiction, Trilling maintained, it is possible to see Forster deliberately chastening his artistic ambition, writing out of what he called a "relaxed will." The frequent arbitrariness of Forster's plotting (he loves to surprise the reader by casually killing off important characters), the ironic tone he favors even when dealing with serious subjects, what Trilling calls his "unbuttoned manner"—all these make it impossible to read Forster with the kind of awe due to his contemporaries Proust and Joyce.

Trilling finds Forster "sometimes irritating in his refusal to be great," and admits that "we now and then wish that the style were less comfortable and more arrogant." But it is precisely Forster's freedom from the arrogant modernist will that makes him so ethically appealing to Trilling, especially in a wartime moment when militant will has made the whole world a battleground. "Greatness in literature, even in comedy, seems to have some affinity with greatness in government and war, suggesting power, a certain sternness, a touch of the imperial and imperious," he writes. "But Forster . . . fears power and suspects formality as the sign of power."

In an introduction to a new edition of *E. M. Forster* written decades later, Trilling explains that in producing the book he was "benefited by the special energies that attend a polemical purpose." This reads like a covert disclaimer, a way of suggesting that with the passing of that polemical purpose, his own enthusiasm for Forster has also waned. And it is striking that the virtues he praises in Forster—casualness, modesty, indifference to power and authority—are conspicuously absent from his own writing. Two of Trilling's favorite words, in fact, are "strenuous" and "exigent," which together make a good summary of the kind of literary sensibility to which Forster is opposed.

Even while writing *E. M. Forster*, Trilling was unable fully to bridge the chasm between his own temperament and his subject's. Appropriately, this difference is most obvious in the chapter on Forster's literary criticism, the ground on which Trilling approaches him not just as a commentator but as a rival practitioner. Writing about Forster the critic, Trilling reveals his distaste for the very qualities he has been praising in Forster the novelist. There is a "great disproportion between Forster's critical gifts and the use he makes of them," Trilling observes, and the disproportion is owed precisely to "an excessive relaxation," which prevents him from making his observations exact and his judgments thorough. The best defense Trilling can make of this "laxness" is that it is "*consciously* a contradiction of the Western tradition of intellect which believes that by making decisions, by choosing precisely, by evaluating correctly it can solve all difficulties." But Trilling cannot quite disguise, from himself or from the reader, his fundamental allegiance to the "tradition of intellect" he praises Forster for abandoning. His own writing is a continuous effort of deciding, choosing, and evaluating; the dignity and occasional pomp of his prose is the stylistic expression of this effortfulness.

The most significant result of Trilling's encounter with Arnold and Forster had less to do with their mistrust of art than with a second, related facet of their achievement: their mistrust of liberalism. If these writers were unable to commit themselves wholly to art, in the way that seems to be requisite for greatness, they were artists enough to be equally unable to commit themselves wholly to liberal dogmas about progress and equality. When Trilling writes of Arnold that "his hatred of reaction was no greater than his hatred of the Philistine liberals who, though they too attacked the old order, betrayed the ideas of true liberalism," we hear an echo of his own predicament in the 1930s.

The second half of *Matthew Arnold* follows its subject's attempts to balance the claims of social justice against the claims of spiritual nobility, the rights of the many against the gifts of the few. To Arnold, as to most of the Victorian sages, the danger of liberal democracy was that it would drown all the high and rare human qualities in a tide of mediocrity. Trilling sees this concern even in Arnold's discussion of an apparently strictly literary matter, like the right way to translate Homer. When Arnold devoted his lectures as Oxford Professor of Poetry to attacking a new English translation of the *Iliad*, it was because the translator's failure to understand Homer's "grand style" helped to reveal "the great defect of English intellect," a lack of nobility. And as Trilling comments, "to lack in nobility is, of course, to fail utterly; it is the peculiarly modern failure;

we begin to see that Arnold's lectures are not merely technical discussions—that, beginning with technique, he is moving by devious ways to a comment on modern life. He is talking about style, and whenever Arnold talks about style he is talking about society."

To say that liberalism fails because of its failure to accommodate or achieve nobility of style, however, would be to make aesthetics more important than ethics; and while some writers might be willing to make this judgment, Trilling is not. Indeed, throughout *Matthew Arnold,* he is torn between sympathy for Arnold's frankly elitist critique of liberalism, and a passionately ethical resentment of that elitism. This comes across most stridently when Trilling discusses Arnold's admiration for the French aphorist Joseph Joubert, who deplored what the 1930s would have called "socially relevant" art: "The disasters of the times and the great scourges of life—hunger, thirst, shame, sickness and death—they can make many tales to draw many tears; but the soul whispers: 'you are hurting me.'" Joubert's preciousness evokes an outburst from Trilling that carries echoes of his early, radical essays: "the only remedies for the deficiencies of such a mind, one feels, would be the hunger, thirst, cold which he excluded from art."

The only way to resolve the deadlock between liberalism and literature would be to discover a way in which the latter actually serves the former—in which art can be considered the accomplice of justice, rather than its seductive rival. And it is this synthesis that Trilling begins to forge in *E. M. Forster,* written four years after *Matthew Arnold.* In Forster, Trilling finds another liberal whose instincts seem to be at war with liberalism: "all his novels are politically and morally tendentious and always in the liberal direction. Yet he is deeply at odds with the liberal mind, and while liberal readers can go a long way with Forster, they can seldom go all the way. . . . They suspect Forster is not quite playing their game; they feel he is challenging *them* as well as what they dislike. And they are right."

Just as Arnold saw the weak point of liberalism in its "style," so, Trilling writes, "for all his long commitment to the doctrines of liberalism, Forster is at war with the liberal imagination." This is the first appearance in Trilling's work of the famous phrase, and in this context it carries a straightforwardly negative charge: the liberal imagination is the failed part of liberalism. "Surely if liberalism has a single desperate weakness," he goes on to say, "it is an inadequacy of imagination: liberalism is always being surprised." It is so surprisable because the right-thinking liberal tends to divide the world into two opposed camps, politically, morally, and socially, and to be sure that he is always on the right side. "We of the liberal connection have always liked to play the old intellectual game of antagonistic principles," Trilling writes, whose "first rule is that if one of two opposed principles is wrong, the other is necessarily right." This certainty that "good is good and bad is bad" means that the liberal does not have to concern himself with all the ways good can produce bad, through unintended consequences, or unacknowledged motives, or fanatical zeal.

It is not hard to see how this criticism would have been applied, by Trilling's first readers, to the fellow-travelling liberals of the 1930s and '40s. This is the type that Trilling criticized in *The Middle of the Journey,* in the characters of Arthur and Nancy Croom. These progressive-minded people are certain that since capitalism and fascism are "bad," the Communist Party and the Soviet Union must be "good," and that their own support for Communism is purely good both in its motives and in its effects. But to Trilling, this particular political dereliction, while dramatic, was only the contemporary expression of a perennial vulnerability in the liberal imagination. It is the same weakness that Forster exposed in his portrait of the Schlegels in *Howards End,* which was published in 1910, long before the Popular Front or even the Soviet Union was dreamed of.

Margaret and Helen Schlegel are examples, Trilling writes, of the way "liberal intellectuals have always moved in an aura of self-congratulation. They sustain themselves by flattering themselves with intentions and they dismiss as 'reactionary' whoever questions them. When the liberal intellectual thinks of himself, he thinks chiefly of his own good will and prefers not to know that the good will generates its own problems, that the love of humanity has its vices and the love of truth its own insensibilities." The fate of Leonard Bast, who is professionally and then physically destroyed by his entanglement with the well-meaning Schlegels, stands as Forster's comment on the danger of well-meaning but unimaginative liberalism.

By demonstrating the weakness of the liberal imagination, however, Forster also seeks to remedy it. As Trilling puts it, his novels are "a kind of mithridate against our being surprised by life." Trilling's name for the homeopathic cure that literature offers to liberalism is "moral realism"—another phrase which would play an important role in his later work. Moral realism "is not the awareness of morality itself but of the contradictions, paradoxes and dangers of living the moral life": it is the understanding that there is no such thing as purity of heart, and that those who believe in their own purity are especially capable of evil.

This knowledge is not merely theoretical, but has the most immediate implications for both personal and political life; and Trilling argues that literature is uniquely able to teach it to us.

> Here is the province of the novelist, for the novelist explores the realm beyond conscious motivation and knows far better than the moralist that an act or a conscious intention may be good at the same time that there is behind it a lack of innocence or an element of self-assertion which, because it is not expressed, makes the act

of virtue either issue in badness or fail of subjective worth. Into this realm law can never penetrate, articulate social judgment cannot go, nor even religion. This is the province of Dostoevsky and Tolstoy, of Henry James, D. H. Lawrence and E. M. Forster, of George Santayana and Aldous Huxley, of all the writers of fiction who are concerned with the question of *style* in morality.

In this way, the opposition of style and morality that had plagued Trilling since the early 1930s is resolved, in a typically dialectical fashion. Style, Arnold and Forster have taught him, is not a luxury, to be dispensed with when crisis comes; rather, style and imagination are the tools with which crisis can be mastered. It follows that the term "liberal imagination," which starts out in Trilling's work as a pejorative, can be reinterpreted, by the time of *The Liberal Imagination,* in a more ambiguous way, as the name now of an ideal, now of the reality that fails to live up to it. This doubleness is announced in the "Preface," when he declares that his goal is "to recall liberalism to its first essential imagination of variousness and possibility, which implies the awareness of complexity and difficulty." His impatience with liberalism has to do with the way it is constantly allowing its "essential imagination" to decay into a complacent failure of imagination.

This danger is implicit in every liberalism, and it is difficult to guard against. One of the charges brought against Cold War liberal anti-Communism, which was coming into its strength just at the time Trilling published *The Liberal Imagination,* is that it allowed its own defense of liberalism to become narrow, singleminded, and bellicose—that is, illiberal. The best reason to deny that Trilling was an intellectual godfather of neoconservatism is that he was aware of this danger, and took care to avoid it in his own work. The key to the lasting power of *The Liberal Imagination* is the way Trilling does not just advocate "variousness" and "complexity," but allows these virtues to structure and animate the book itself. In this, Trilling makes an advantage out of what is often a defect in essay collections—the different perspectives, vocabularies, and occasions that make the individual parts fail to cohere into a whole. In *The Liberal Imagination,* the perpetual restatement of the liberal dilemma, always in slightly different terms, helps prevent it from ossifying into a formula.

One of the tenets of Trilling's liberalism is that the writer's individual will is, ultimately, of service to the greater good. Yet he never slights the sheer, splendid selfishness of that will, the way it makes a "large, strict, personal demand on life," as he writes in a seldom quoted but revealing essay on F. Scott Fitzgerald. The Fitzgerald of the 1920s represented just the kind of writer the liberals of the 1930s turned against—lyrical and romantic, rich and an observer of the rich. Yet Trilling insists that Fitzgerald's unguarded desire for money and fame is part of the same ardent ambition that made him "heroic": "Fitzgerald was perhaps the last notable writer to affirm the Romantic fantasy, descended from the Renaissance, of personal ambition and heroism." If you censure this kind of worldly ambition in Fitzgerald, Trilling reminds the reader, you will also have to censure Shakespeare, Dickens, and "those fabricators of the honorific 'de,' Voltaire and Balzac." What redeems the egotism of the novelist is the egolessness of the novel, which at its height, Trilling writes, is always an expression of "love." Fitzgerald's "first impulse was to love the good, and we know this the more surely because we perceive that he loved the good not only with his mind but also with his quick senses and his youthful pride and desire."

For Trilling, however, the best example of this kind of love is found in Henry James, the novelist so revered by the modernists in general and the New York intellectuals in particular. Starting with the very first essay in the book, "Reality in America," James is the test case for Trilling's insistence that liberalism and literature can be reconciled, appearances to the contrary notwithstanding. To mainstream liberal opinion, whose canonical expression Trilling finds in V. L. Parrington's *Main Currents in American Thought,* James is a suspect figure: as an aesthete and an expatriate, he is doubly vulnerable to the charge of escapism. "By liberal critics," Trilling writes, "James is traditionally put to the ultimate question: of what use, of what actual political use, are his gifts and their intention?" He contrasts this suspicion of James with the liberal admiration for the naturalism of Theodore Dreiser, despite all his faults of style and intellect: "It is as if wit, and flexibility of mind, and perception, and knowledge were to be equated with aristocracy and political reaction, while dullness and stupidity must naturally suggest a virtuous democracy."

It is to refute this accusation, against James in particular and imaginative literature in general, that Trilling writes the essay that is the book's *summa*, "The Princess Casamassima." The choice of subject is itself polemical: this novel, published in 1886, takes place far from James's usual fictional precincts of Anglo-American high society. Rather, its hero is a poor bookbinder, Hyacinth Robinson, who is drawn into a revolutionary conspiracy and ordered to carry out a terrorist assassination. James, Trilling means to remind the reader, was perfectly capable of dealing with the explicitly political themes that Thirties liberals thought fiction should embrace. In fact, as Trilling shows in an excursus on nineteenth-century anarchism, James's portrait of the world of working-class radicalism was far more accurate than his contemporaries were willing to give him credit for. James belongs to the twentieth century, rather than the Victorian age, in what he called his "imagination of disaster," his ability to "see life as ferocious and sinister."

Yet *The Princess Casamassima* resists the expectations of the self-congratulatory progressive reader. For one thing, it does not portray its oppressed working-class characters as saintly or innocent, in the Popular Front manner of a writer like John Steinbeck. "The literature of our liberal democracy," Trilling writes, "pets and dandles its underprivileged characters, and, quite as if it had the right to do so, forgives them what faults they have." This was a perpetual complaint of Trilling's, which he took pains to avoid in his own fiction. In *The Middle of the Journey*, the Crooms are constantly making excuses for the derelictions of the handyman Duck Caldwell, whom John Laskell sees to be actually vicious and debased. Trilling's short story "The Other Margaret" revolves around the inability of a well-meaning middle-class girl to acknowledge her own dislike of her family's black maid: "She's not responsible," the young Margaret says about her namesake. " 'It's not her fault. She couldn't help it. Society—' But at that big word she halted, unable to handle it. 'We can't blame her,' she said, defiantly but a little lamely."

In *The Princess Casamassima,* Trilling points to the character of Rosy Muniment as an example of James's impartiality, which is based on a truly democratic sense of each character's equal autonomy. Rosy is an impoverished but courageous invalid, a figure whom the reader feels ought to be admired, yet she is also manipulative and cruel, and "the revelation . . . that we don't have to" like her "is an emotional relief and a moral enlightenment." The same clearsightedness has more directly political uses, too, as Trilling shows when he discusses the relationship between Paul Muniment, the radical leader, and the titular Princess, a wealthy American woman estranged from her Italian husband. James makes clear that Paul's idealism coexists with intense personal ambition, and that the Princess's quest for what she calls the "real" and the "solid" leads her to use fantasies of political violence as a form of therapy and penance.

Here is James's demonstration of what Trilling described as "moral realism," the study of "the contradictions, paradoxes and dangers of living the moral life." For Trilling, the Princess is the classic example of what a later generation would be taught, by Tom Wolfe, to call "radical chic": "a perfect drunkard of reality, she is ever drawn to look for stronger and stronger drams." In other words, she has fallen victim to what Trilling called "the chronic American belief that there exists an opposition between reality and mind and that one must enlist oneself in the party of reality."

But reality, as Hyacinth Robinson comes to understand, is not simply restricted to the physical or sociological. Mind is itself a reality, sometimes the most important one. Hyacinth is the illegitimate son of an English aristocrat and the French courtesan who ended up murdering him—a rather gaudy backstory, as Trilling acknowledges, but also an allegorical one. Through his mother, Hyacinth is the heir to poverty and exclusion, and to the working-class solidarity that leads him to become radicalized. Through his father, however, he has an equal, though unrecognized, claim on the world's best things—including art and literature, for which he develops an unsatisfied passion. This double heritage is what allows Hyacinth to see the relationship between beauty and justice as not simply a rivalry, but a dialectic. As Trilling puts it, "he recognizes that 'the fabric of civilization as we know it' is inextricably bound up with this injustice: the monuments of art and learning and taste have been reared upon coercive power."

This is as powerful an indictment of culture as the one made by Walter Benjamin in "Theses on the Philosophy of History": "There is no document of civilization which is not at the same time a document of barbarism." In fact, Trilling goes even further than Benjamin, insisting that it is not just "civilization" that is complicit with injustice, but the artist himself, thanks to the insistent will that Trilling writes about so often—what he calls here "the superbness and arbitrariness of great spirits." If Hyacinth is a hero, it is because he feels the claims of each side of this dialectic: he believes that the fabric of civilization deserves to be ripped apart, and he believes that it must be preserved at any cost. That is why, when he is finally ordered to attack civilization head-on, by committing murder, he ends up taking his own life instead: "embodying two ideals at once," Trilling writes, "he takes upon himself, in full consciousness, the guilt of each."

To say that the logical result of James's "moral realism" is suicide, of course, is not exactly a confident retort to the question Trilling asked in "Reality in America": "of what use, of what actual political use, are his gifts and their intention?" But in his essay on *The Princess Casamassima,* Trilling makes clear that what makes James stronger than his creation Hyacinth is his ability to "embody two ideals at once" and still live—indeed, to flourish. In a passage that seems designed to demonstrate the proper use of Freudian interpretation, Trilling discusses a dream of James's, in which the writer was assailed by a nameless presence and tried to shut the door against it. He then realized "that I, in my appalled state, was more appalling than that awful agent, creature, or presence," opened the door, and chased down the enemy that had been chasing him.

"One needs to be a genius to counter-attack nightmare: perhaps this is the definition of genius," Trilling remarks. Art is the form in which the writer, and through him the reader, can face down the intolerable contradictions of history. This is because art begins in will, but ends in love: as with Fitzgerald, Trilling insists that James's "power to tell the truth arises from [his] power of love." James's love of his freely created characters, his refusal to divide them neatly into good and bad, denies readers any reassurance that "good is good and bad is bad." But it gives the liberal imagination what it actually needs much more. James is able, in Trilling's words, to tell "us the truth in a single luminous act of creation." Truth, not justice, is the end of art, but Trilling has the liberal faith that justice cannot exist without truth. For this reason, even a writer as apparently aloof from politics as Henry James performs an indispensable public function.

It is in this essay that Trilling makes the observation quoted earlier, "It is one of the necessities of successful modern story that the author shall have somewhere entrusted his personal fantasy to the tale"; and Trilling is to be found in his essay on *The Princess Casamassima* as surely as James is to be found in the novel. Trilling's own travails as a novelist can be glimpsed in his understanding of the artist's aggressive ambition. His brief but formative period as a radical shows in his sympathy with Hyacinth's revolutionary plans, and his still greater sympathy with the intellectual conscience that interferes with those plans. His study of Arnold and Forster made it possible for him to understand his own strictures against the liberal imagination as a means of strengthening, rather than defaming, liberalism. James's fiction is, of course, a greater and more primary achievement than Trilling's criticism; but the critic and the novelist do not finally belong to different realms.

At the same time that it demonstrates the essentially literary nature of his critical intelligence, this essay, like *The Liberal Imagination* as a whole, shows how central Trilling is— or should be—to our understanding of the main project of postwar liberal thought: a renewed commitment to pluralism. Trilling, thinking through the medium of literature rather than history or political philosophy, reaches the same kinds of conclusions that can be found in the work of Isaiah Berlin and Hannah Arendt. From Hyacinth Robinson, he learns that not all human goods can be measured on the same scale, that the claims of art and those of justice are incommensurable (though not necessarily incompatible). From Henry James, he learns that the preservation of human difference, the ability to imagine opposing characters with equal sympathy, is the greatest expression of love. If the basic principles of liberalism today are the renunciation of utopianism and the sanctity of diversity, then Trilling deserves to be credited as one of liberalism's most profound expositors. As long as these principles are honored, *The Liberal Imagination* will be a book that matters; and if they should ever cease to be honored, it will matter all the more.

4 isaac babel and the rabbis

When *The Middle of the Journey* was published, one of the criticisms it provoked was that Trilling had erred in not making his characters Jewish. The intellectual circles in which Trilling moved in the 1930s and 1940s, where he found the originals of figures like the Crooms and John Laskell, were largely made up of Jews; while he taught at Columbia, then still a Protestant bastion, Trilling published his essays in *Partisan Review* and *Commentary,* the house organs of the New York Jewish intellectuals. Yet "not one of the essential characters is, incredibly, a Jew," complained Leslie Fiedler, "though much of the flavor of the Communist experience in America is their flavor."

This may not be entirely correct. There is, in fact, a glancing allusion to Jewishness in the novel, when John Laskell, the character who comes closest to being the author's proxy, is quizzed about his name by his British nurse, Miss Paine. " 'It sounds quite English,' Miss Paine said. She spoke it again, as if testing it. 'John Laskell,' she said. 'It sounds like a Lancashire name. Are you English?' . . . No, he was not English. There was a modification he might make—his mother had been born in the first year of his grandparents' long English visit. But that did not make her English, or him." It is Trilling's own history: his grandparents had emigrated from Eastern Europe to England before moving finally to New York. It seems that, like his creator, Laskell bears a Jewish name that happens to function as Anglo-Saxon camouflage.

The sound of his name helped Trilling early in his career, when he was the first Jew to be hired by the Columbia English Department. As Diana Trilling dryly observed in her memoir, *The Beginning of the Journey,* "Had his name been that of his maternal grandfather, Israel Cohen, it is highly questionable whether the offer would have been made." As things were, it was hard enough for Trilling to fit in at Columbia: after his appointment, a senior professor told him openly that "it was his hope that Lionel's appointment would not be used to open the department to other Jews." But the very Englishness of Trilling's name also raised suspicions that it must have been adopted as a disguise—a corollary, perhaps, to Trilling's love of English literature and his reserved demeanor.

In fact, Trilling went through life with the name his father and grandfather bore—unlike many New York intellectuals, whose family names really had been changed to sound less Jewish. (Diana Trilling writes that he "was much interested in the origin of the name but was never able to determine its source with certainty. It was perhaps the name of a town in the Polish Corridor or associated with the resort town of Wassertrilling in Austria.") Yet the suspicion of trying to "pass" does not attach itself to, say, Irving Howe (born Horenstein). To Alfred Kazin, part of Trilling's mystique came from the way he seemed "to be a Jew and yet not Jewish"—Jewish, here, functioning as a token of immigrant poverty, of the kind Kazin wrote about in his memoir *A Walker in the City.* "For Trilling I would always be 'too Jewish,' too full of my lower class experience. He would always defend himself from the things he had left behind," Kazin wrote, himself sounding a little defensive. It would be hard to tell from this description that, as Diana Trilling explained, Trilling's father was a tailor, and he grew up in circumstances nearly as humble as Kazin's.

Yet it is true that Trilling expressed strong resistance to being described as a Jewish writer. In 1944, he was asked to contribute to a symposium in the *Contemporary Jewish Record,* a magazine that was the predecessor to *Commentary,* on the subject of "American Literature and the Younger Generation of American Jews." His short essay, republished in later collections as "Under Forty," comprehensively declines any Jewish identification, in a way that seems strange and even suspect in our own confidently multicultural age. Trilling may feel it to be a "point of honor" to acknowledge his Jewishness, to make clear that "I would not, even if I could, deny or escape being Jewish"—a gesture of solidarity that is morally imperative in the year 1944, with "the Jewish situation as bad as it is." But this kind of Jewishness is strictly formal, not substantive, and Trilling insists, "I cannot discover anything in my professional intellectual life which I can specifically trace back to my Jewish birth and rearing. I do not think of myself as a 'Jewish writer.' I do not have it in mind to serve by my writing any Jewish purpose. I should resent it if a critic of my work were to discover in it either faults or virtues which he called Jewish."

This repudiation is all the more striking given that, as Trilling goes on to explain in the same essay, he actually began his career as an editor and writer for a Jewish magazine, *The Menorah Journal.* This publication was edited in the 1920s by Elliot Cohen, who would go on to found *Commentary* in 1945, and it attracted an impressive group of young contributors. Some of Trilling's earliest criticism, collected after his death in *Speaking of Literature and Society,* appeared in this Jewish venue, and dealt directly with Jewish subjects. Yet he remembered the magazine, and the effort at "Jewish self-realization" that it represented, as being "sterile at best."

In this retrospective judgment, he is quite faithful to the way he felt and wrote even at the time. In a review published in *Menorah Journal* in 1929, Trilling was already impatient with the way Jewish novelists wrote as though being Jewish, and accepting one's Jewishness, is an interesting accomplishment in itself. "As soon as the Jewish writer gets his hero to be a Jew," Trilling complains, "he wraps him up warm in a *talith* and puts him away. . . . the Jewish hero is lifted out of life and made to goggle his eyes in functionless ecstasy at the fact that he is a Jew." Trilling insists that the Jewish novel is in need of "poetry, passion, a little madness. It will support greatness." It's as though he were looking forward to the very writers, like Bellow and Mailer, whose triumphant "mishagass" or craziness he would later envy.

But American Jewish writing in the 1920s was not what it would become in the 1950s. In the era of Mann, Proust, and Eliot, Trilling had little time for a literature that boasted Ludwig Lewisohn as its brightest light. On the other hand, Trilling was too intellectually rigorous to believe that he could be nourished by the legacy of Judaism, when he knew almost nothing about it. It is not unusual for secular Jewish literary critics to wonder if their profession is just the latest incarnation of the Judaic intellectual tradition—the Talmudic tradition—with its emphasis on textual explication and intellectual controversy. Harold Rosenberg, one of the leading New York intellectuals, felt legitimated by the notion that "For two thousand years the main energies of Jewish communities . . . have gone into the mass production of intellectuals." But Trilling, precisely because he respected the legacy of Judaism, refused to make a spurious claim to it: "I can have no pride in seeing a long tradition, often great and heroic, reduced to this small status in me," he wrote in "Under Forty."

Trilling's intellectual life, he already saw in the 1920s, would lie among the great works of English literature; and while this literature could be Christian, post-Christian, or secular, it was virtually never Jewish. This was the discovery he confirmed to himself in an essay he wrote in 1930 but didn't publish, "The Changing Myth of the Jew." This study of the treatment of Jews and Judaism in English literature, from Chaucer to George Eliot, is not one of Trilling's important works; in fact, it is surprisingly cursory and disengaged. But then, the verdict of the essay is that English literature has never truly engaged with the Jews, even when it claims to portray them. "The Jew in fiction," Trilling concludes with some irritation, "was always an abstraction, a symbol, a racial stereotype created by men whose chief concern was obviously much less to tell the truth about the character of the Jew than it was to serve their own political and economic interests and their own emotional needs. In short, the Jew in English fiction is a myth."

Where Trilling differs from most Jewish readers, certainly today, is in denying that the prevalence of this malign myth has any effect on the way that a Jew encounters English fiction. A myth, Trilling judges severely, is simply an untruth, a non-being; and the only thing to do with a non-being is ignore it. "What importance has an account of material which is confessedly merely mythological? The importance to the historian, the psychologist, the sociologist, the political thinker is obvious. But to one interested chiefly in literature, the answer is not so plain." Perhaps his failure to publish the essay represents Trilling's final judgment on the whole subject. The question of a specifically Jewish perspective on English literature is just not worth talking about.

In this refusal of a parochial attitude toward universal questions—political as well as literary—Trilling was typical of the Jewish writers associated with *Partisan Review.* Looking back on his early Jewish milieu from an even greater distance, in the 1970s, he valued it mainly for leading him, indirectly, to a broader, quasi-Marxist perspective: "The discovery, through the *Menorah Journal,* of the Jewish situation had the effect of making society at last available to my imagination. It made America available to my imagination. . . . One couldn't, for example, think for very long about Jews without perceiving that one was using the category of social class."

The irony, of course, is that in their very repudiation of Jewishness, writers like Trilling, Howe, Clement Greenberg, Philip Rahv, and the whole New York intellectual circle were making a universalist gesture that appears, in retrospect, as the very insignia of their Jewishness. By 1973, Philip Rieff, in his eccentric polemic against the spirit of the 1960s called *Fellow Teachers,* could identify Trilling as the archetypal "Jew of culture"—Trilling, who had started out denying that his Jewishness and his culture had anything to do with one another.

But this denial was less absolute than Trilling sometimes made it sound. It is hardly an accident that, in two of his most personal and suggestive essays, Trilling approached modern literature from an explicitly Jewish perspective. Indeed, in both "Isaac Babel" (1955) and "Wordsworth and the Rabbis" (1950), Trilling enlists Jewishness as a central metaphor—perhaps even an explanation—for his divided feelings about the modern spirit, the very division that is the theme and engine of his criticism.

"Isaac Babel," which Trilling wrote as an introduction to an edition of Babel's stories, starts out by remarking on the "disturbing" effect that *Red Cavalry* had on him when he first read it in 1929. Part of the "shock," Trilling explains, came from the stories' "energy and boldness"—the wrenched, garish imagery and the immersion in violence that still make Babel challenging today. Another part had to do with the ideological climate of the period, when "one still spoke of the 'Russian experiment'": to liberal intellectuals like Trilling, Babel's revelation of the savagery that built the Soviet state was unnerving.

But the most personal source of disturbance, and the element that Trilling makes the focus of his essay, was Babel's interpretation of Jewishness. In the same year that Trilling lodged his complaint about the sterility of American Jewish fiction, he found in Babel an infinitely more vital and relevant treatment of Jewish identity. *Red Cavalry* tells, in short, fragmentary episodes, the story of Babel's experiences in the Red Army during the Soviet-Polish war of 1920, when he served as a war correspondent with the front-line cavalry troops of Marshal Budyonny. Babel's position as a writer and intellectual among violent, often bestial soldiers was only made more uncomfortable by the fact that he was a Jew, while his comrades were Cossacks—traditionally the worst persecutors of the Jews of Russia.

As Trilling writes, "a Jew in a Cossack regiment was more than an anomaly, it was a joke, for between Cossack and Jew there existed not merely hatred but a polar opposition"—a difference not just of ethnicity, but of values. As Trilling summarizes it, "The Jew conceived his own ideal character to consist in his being intellectual, pacific, humane. The Cossack was physical, violent, without mind or manners." Of course, this summary of the Jewish character by no means accounts for the full variety of Jewish life in Eastern Europe, or even in Babel's own fiction. His "Odessa Stories" show that the same contrast between violence and intellect could just as well exist within the Jewish community: the heroes of those grotesque comic tales are Jewish gangsters, whose huge appetites and casual cruelty rival those of the Cossacks in *Red Cavalry*.

But this Jewish myth—unlike the malign Jewish myths he encountered in English literature—seemed to Trilling a valuable one, because it expressed something of his own temperament and aspirations. He writes poetically about Babel's face, as seen in a snapshot: "the face is very long and thin, charged with emotion and internality; bitter, intense, very sensitive, touched with humor, full of consciousness and contradiction. It is 'typically' an intellectual's face, a scholar's face, and it has great charm. I should not want to speak of it as a Jewish face, but it is a kind of face which many Jews used to aspire to have, or hoped their sons would have."

What does it mean for this lovingly described Jewish ideal, then, that Babel seems so often to ridicule and abase precisely those qualities in himself that Trilling admires? *Red Cavalry* is constantly observing the contrast between the tenderheartedness of Lyutov, Babel's narrator and alter ego, and the coarseness of the troops he rides with. The Cossacks in these stories are usually to be found feuding over horses, raping women, and massacring civilians—especially Jews. In the story "Zamosc," a fellow-soldier, not knowing that he is talking to a Jew, tells Lyutov: "The Jew is guilty before all men. . . . There will be very few of them left when the war is over."

But even as he is depicting scenes that seem designed to make the reader loathe the Cossacks, Babel himself seems to envy them, and to despise the ethical scruples that prevent him from emulating them. His most famous story, "My First Goose," shows him winning the respect of the soldiers—who at first despise him because of his Jewish-intellectual glasses—by seizing and killing an old peasant woman's goose. In "Argamak," he is given a spirited horse that has been confiscated from a Cossack officer, and shows himself unequal to riding it: "I wore out his back. It became covered in sores. Metallic flies fed on those sores. Hoops of coagulated black blood girdled the horse's belly." Argamak's wounds are the stigmata of the narrator's unmanliness. At the end of the story, this physical ineptitude is shown to have a moral dimension as well, when the narrator complains that it is unfair of Argamak's previous owner to consider him a personal enemy. After all, he didn't ask for the Cossack's horse to be taken away: "How am I to blame?" he asks the squadron commander. This whine provokes a famous rebuke, which Trilling quotes: "I understand you completely. . . . Your aim is to live without making enemies. . . . Everything you do is aimed that way—so you won't have any enemies."

From the perspective Trilling describes as ideally Jewish, the desire to have no enemies is laudable, since it means wanting to live in peace and commit no offenses. From the Cossack perspective, it is contemptible: everyone has enemies, and the only honorable way to respond to them is to fight them. The imperative of self-help and martial readiness, in fact, has something in common with the Zionist message, which was spreading through Eastern Europe during the years of Babel's youth—especially in Odessa, the cosmopolitan Russian city where he was born in 1894. The Hebrew poet Chaim Nachman Bialik was living in Odessa when he wrote his great poem "In the City of Slaughter," which bitterly condemned Jewish men for failing to fight back against Russian pogroms.

But it is not simply physical courage, Trilling insists, that Babel finds admirable in the Cossacks. It is, rather, the quality of "noble savagery" that Tolstoy had found in them, their "primitive energy, passion, and virtue." If the Jew was the man of the mind and the book, the Cossack was "the man of the body—and of the horse, the man who moved with speed and grace." At moments, Trilling shows, Babel sounds enraptured with the sheer height and strength and good looks of the soldiers, especially as contrasted with the slight, hunched, timid Jews he is constantly encountering.

Yet if *Red Cavalry* simply endorsed the Cossack and condemned the Jew, it would hardly possess what Trilling called the "intensity, irony, and ambiguousness" that made it so disturbing. Babel may seem to want to emulate the Cossack, yet it is unmistakable that, in his campaign through Poland, he is constantly drawn to Jews. In "The Rebbe," he has Shabbat dinner at the court of a Hasidic rabbi in Zhitomir. In "The Cemetery in Kozin" he records the epitaphs for dead sages: "Wolf, son of Elijah, prince abducted from the Torah in his nineteenth spring." These two moments converge in "The Rebbe's Son," where the writer encounters Ilya, the son of the Zhitomir Rebbe, who himself has been abducted from the Torah—in his case, because he has become a Communist and joined the Red Army. When Ilya dies, his trunk is made a symbol of the irreconcilability of scholar and soldier: "Portraits of Lenin and Maimonides lay side by side. Lenin's nodulous skull and the tarnished silk of the portraits of Maimonides. . . . in the margins of communist leaflets swarmed crooked lines of Ancient Hebrew verse."

To Trilling, the artist of the dialectic, it is exactly Babel's refusal to grant victory to one of his warring ideals that makes him a great writer: "the opposition of these two images made his art." Specifically, it is what made him a great modernist writer. When he first read Babel, Trilling recalls, he was "afraid of the literature of modern Europe, because I was scared of its terrible intensities, and ironies, and ambiguities." To appreciate modernism, it is necessary to feel the attraction of violence as well as peace, of transgression as well as order. One of the major purposes of Trilling's criticism, in fact, is to keep the antinomian potential of modern literature alive in the reader's consciousness—to combat what he calls "the museum knowingness about art . . . our consumer's pride in buying only the very best spiritual commodities." To respond to the horror and confusion in *Red Cavalry* with knowingness is to avoid genuinely encountering it, while the "moments when we lack the courage to confront, or the strength to endure, some particular work of art" may be those in which we encounter it most authentically.

In a culture that takes literary transgression for granted, in fact, the greatest shock may come from literature that refuses to transgress. That is Trilling's premise in "Wordsworth and the Rabbis," his other most explicitly Jewish essay. Written for the centenary of Wordsworth's death, the essay tries to identify the quality in the poet that makes him "unacceptable to the modern world," to find out "why . . . he is often thought to be rather absurd and even a little despicable." This technique, in which his contemporaries' failure to respond to a certain writer is made to serve as a diagnosis of the age, is one of Trilling's most fruitful. It is also one of the important uses of the rhetorical "we": when Trilling asks why "we" no longer appreciate Wordsworth, he is both acknowledging his part in that antipathy, and inviting the reader to admit his or her own.

What is uncharacteristic in this essay is the way Trilling pivots, almost immediately, from Wordsworth's poetry to another text, which has no apparent relation to it: the *Pirke Aboth,* usually rendered in English as the "Ethics of the Fathers." This is, as Trilling describes it, "a collection of maxims and *pensées*" from the rabbinic sages of the first centuries C.E. It is the only traditional Jewish text that Trilling writes about in the whole body of his work, and he is conscious enough of the anomaly to offer an explanation of how he became acquainted with it. As a boy, he recalls, "when I was supposed to be reading my prayers —very long, and in the Hebrew language, which I never mastered—I spent the required time and made it seem that I was doing my duty by reading the English translation of the *Pirke Aboth* . . . included in the prayerbook. It was more attractive to me than psalms, meditations, and supplications; it seemed more humane, and the Fathers had a curious substantiality."

Once again, Trilling is scrupulous in setting out the limits of his claim to Jewishness: he even manages to make his knowledge of the *Pirke Aboth* evidence of a larger failure to learn about Judaism. Nor does he take much account of the historical background of its composition—above all, the destruction of the Temple in Jerusalem, in 70 C.E., which turned Judaism from a national and priestly religion into a diasporic and rabbinical one. This context, in which the rabbis tried to sustain Judaism in the face of defeat and exile, helps to explain the feature of the work that most intrigues Trilling—its unworldliness, its principled lack of interest in power.

Trilling barely touches on this history in "Wordsworth and the Rabbis." But then, if he were a more conventional literary historian, he would never have made such an unlikely conjunction in the first place. He is, in fact, not entirely at ease with his own justification for reading Wordsworth through the lens of *Pirke Aboth,* which is that "the quality in Wordsworth that now makes him unacceptable is a Judaic quality." But this assertion, unintelligible as it might be in objective, historical terms, becomes meaningful when it is read subjectively, as an expression of Trilling's own experience as a reader. Really, the essay is an attempt to identify a certain quality of sensibility that Trilling finds in both Wordsworth and the Rabbis, a sensibility whose common denominator is not Judaism but Trilling himself. As always in his criticism, the logic of the essay is that of the movements of Trilling's own mind, as it resists and embraces a text.

In this case, the quality that Trilling calls "Judaic" is closely related to the one that he called Jewish in the Babel essay, and once again he defines it by contrast: "We find in the tractate no implication of moral struggle. We find the energy of assiduity but not the energy of resistance." Above all, he writes, "there is no mention in the *Aboth* of courage or heroism. . . . There is not a word to suggest that the life of virtue and religious devotion requires the heroic quality." The incompatibility of the Jewish and the heroic—which also meant, to Trilling, the "direct, immediate, fierce"—was what Babel deplored. Trilling sympathizes with him, and in "Wordsworth and the Rabbis," too, he admits to finding the rabbis' lack of interest in "moral struggle" discomfiting: "as much as anything in my boyhood experience of the *Aboth* it was this that fascinated me. It also repelled me."

It is this mixed reaction that makes Trilling think of the *Aboth* in conjunction with Wordsworth, whose poetry also makes modern readers uncomfortable. The reason, he suggests, is that both propose a life in which piety—with all its implications of submission, reverence, and quietness—is the supreme virtue. To Wordsworth, Nature is beneficent and all-sufficient, and a being in communion with Nature has no need of heroic efforts: "the soul / Seeks for no trophies, struggles for no spoils / That may attest her prowess, blest in thoughts / That are their own perfection and reward, / Strong in herself and in beatitude," Trilling quotes from "The Prelude."

It may seem perverse for Trilling to insist on a resemblance between this quasi-pantheism and the faith of the rabbis, which is aggressively uninterested in nature. In chapter three of the *Aboth,* for instance, Rabbi Yaakov is quoted as saying: "One who walks along a road and studies, and interrupts his studying to say, 'How beautiful is this tree!', 'How beautiful is this ploughed field!'—the Torah considers it as if he had forfeited his life." How to reconcile this with the poet who wrote, "One impulse from a vernal wood / May teach you more of man, / Of moral evil and of good, / Than all the sages can"?

What they have in common, Trilling suggests, is the sensibility Wordsworth captured in the phrase "wise passiveness." Such passiveness is not resignation or apathy, but rather a faith that the world has been ordered for man's good, so that we do not have to conquer our place in it, but simply accept the place we have been given. As Trilling puts it, "different as the immediately present objects were in each case, Torah for the Rabbis, Nature for Wordsworth, there existed for the Rabbis and for Wordsworth a great object, which is from God and may be said to represent Him as a sort of surrogate."

What breathes in the *Aboth* is the Rabbis' absolute certainty that a life devoted to Torah is the best life. "Exile yourself to a place of Torah," advises one of them, "do not say that it will come after you." The rabbis are aware that the life of study has its own pitfalls, and they warn against intellectual vanity, quarrelsomeness, and the temptation to elevate theory over practice. But they are certain that no worldly activity can rival the study of the Law, and they warn against every kind of distraction: "one who speaks excessively brings on sin"; "one who excessively converses with a woman causes evil to himself, neglects the study of Torah, and in the end inherits purgatory"; "desire not the table of kings, for your table is greater than theirs, and your crown is greater than theirs." The whole ethos of the *Pirke Aboth* is encapsulated in its very first line, which advises: "Be cautious in judgment. Establish many pupils. And make a fence around the Torah."

It is this fencing off of so much of life that both repels and fascinates Trilling, since it seems to rule out the aggression and ambition from which modern literature is made. What would that literature be without its interest in sex, power, and self-expression? Don't the great modern novelists and poets celebrate the will, and use art to assert their own wills? "The predilection for the powerful, the fierce, the assertive, the personally militant is very strong in our culture," Trilling remarks, citing everyone from Yeats and Lawrence to Ayn Rand ("that curious underground work *The Fountainhead*").

Only by turning away from this literature, which informs modern assumptions so deeply, is it possible to see that an alternative exists. This is what Trilling calls the "sentiment of Being," the feeling that the world does not have to be remade or struggled for, because it already is, and is good. Happiness is a matter not of becoming, but of being; not of creating, but of studying, whether we study "sermons in stones" or pages of the Talmud. Once again, it is clear, Trilling has made Jewishness the name of a way of being that is "pacific and humane," and that stands opposed to a seemingly more attractive way that is "fierce" and "militant." Only now it is not the Cossack who represents that seductive vitalism, but modern literature itself—the very modernism that counts Babel as one of its greatest artists, and Trilling as one of its greatest interpreters. To be Jewish, for Trilling, is to stand both inside and outside the modern, to embrace its liberations and mourn its casualties. Or perhaps—since Trilling warned against finding in his work any specifically Jewish "faults or virtues"—to stand inside and outside the modern was Trilling's own destiny as a writer; and everything in his life, from his ambition as a novelist to his identity as a Jew, was made to serve it.

5 a syllabus of terrors

In 1967, Trilling edited *The Experience of Literature,* an anthology for college students. He chose to represent Isaac Babel in this volume not by one of his most famous and representative stories—the obvious choice would have been "My First Goose"—but by the brief "Di Grasso," one of Babel's tales of his Odessa childhood. In "Di Grasso," the Jew-Cossack opposition does not appear—there are no soldiers to be seen, and the Jewishness of the milieu, though taken for granted, hardly matters for the story Babel wants to tell. Here, instead, he finds a new embodiment of savage, thrilling, amoral energy: the actor, who serves as a representative of the artist in general.

In the story, the fourteen-year-old narrator is working as a ticket-seller for a theatrical producer, who has hired Di Grasso, a Sicilian actor, to star in a series of plays, including Shakespeare. The performance Babel writes about, however, is "a Sicilian folk drama, a story as ordinary as the alternation of night and day"—a trite melodrama about a shepherd whose fiancée is stolen by a city slicker. The play is shaping up to be a disaster—"Dead as a doornail," the producer laments at intermission—before it suddenly comes to life in the very last scene. Babel describes how Di Grasso, as the cuckolded shepherd, attacks his hated rival: "he smiled, rose into the air, flew across the stage of the municipal theatre, landed on Giovanni's shoulders and, biting his throat right through, growling and looking from side to side, began to suck the blood from the wound."

This cannibalistic leap, which Babel describes as a kind of magic levitation—later, he writes that Di Grasso is "detached from the earth by an unfathomable force"—turns out to be the making of the play. Di Grasso is acclaimed as "the most remarkable actor of the century," and tickets start selling "at five times their asking price." It is also this leap that drew Trilling to the story, as he explains in the preface he wrote for the anthology. In his eyes, it represents the way a feat of artistry can serve as "an intimation of the possibility of freedom from the bondage of our human condition," and in particular from "the constraints of society, from the dullness, the passivity, the acquiescence in which we live most of our lives."

The very simplicity of the leap—the fact that it is a bodily, athletic achievement, not a mental one—makes it a perfect metaphor for Trilling's sense that the allure of art has more to do with energy than with intellection. Babel himself seems to say as much when he writes that "on this visit to our town Di Grasso played *King Lear, Othello,*" and other masterpieces, "asserting with each word and movement that in the frenzy of noble passion there is more justice and hope than in the joyless principles of the world." The implication seems to be that Shakespeare's intricately wrought plays say no more, at bottom, than Di Grasso's leap: that poetry and drama are just expansions of the basic feeling of "frenzy" and "passion" that are found, in purest form, in a graceful jump and a murderous bite. In this image, Babel vindicates Nietzsche's understanding of the Dionysian spirit of art, as formulated in *The Birth of Tragedy:* "In song and in dance man expresses himself as a member of a higher community; he has forgotten how to walk and speak and is on the way toward flying in the air, dancing."

If this is true, it would mean that art has more in common with violence than with justice, with the Cossack than with the Jew. The excitement and threat of modernism is that it makes this proposition so plausible. "Nothing is more characteristic of modern literature than its discovery and canonization of the primal, nonethical energies," Trilling writes. So self-evident is this point that, on several occasions, Trilling enforces it simply by listing the modernist masters that he and his generation idolized: "Yeats and Eliot, Proust and Joyce, Lawrence and Gide," runs the catalog in "The Meaning of a Literary Idea"; in "The Function of the Little Magazine," the list is expanded to "Proust, Joyce, Lawrence, Eliot, Yeats, Mann (in his creative work), Kafka, Rilke, Gide." Each time he mentions these writers, it is to underscore their ethical dubiety: "all have their own love of justice and the good life, but in not one of them does it take the form of a love of the ideas and emotions which liberal democracy, as known by our educated class, has declared respectable."

The point was significant because, to readers of Trilling's generation, these modernist writers had a more than literary authority. They were what he described as "*figures*—that is to say, creative spirits whose work requires an especially conscientious study because in it are to be discerned significances, even mysteries, even powers, which carry it beyond what in a loose and general sense we call literature, beyond even what we think of as very good literature, and bring it as close to an approximation of sacred wisdom as can be achieved in our culture." No one who has read the New Critics explicating a text by Eliot, or the passionate defenses of modernism that filled *Partisan Review* in the late 1930s, will suspect Trilling of exaggerating here. Certainly, Trilling considered his own literary intelligence to have been deeply shaped by the modernists of the 1920s, the golden age that began when he was a teenager. "Taking the cue of W. H. Auden's remark that a real book reads us," he writes, "I have been read by Eliot's poems and by *Ulysses* and by *Remembrance of Things Past* and by *The Castle* for a good many years now, since early youth. . . . Their nature is such that our relationship has been very intimate."

Perhaps the most surprising fact about Trilling's work, then, is that not one of his major essays deals with any of the novelists and poets he names in these repeated lists. The reader will look in vain for Trilling's thoughts on Mann or Kafka or Gide, and his pieces on Eliot and Joyce (neither collected by him in a book) do not engage with their most important work. How to explain this omission, which is so complete that it could not possibly be accidental? The contrast with Edmund Wilson, for instance, is striking. Wilson made his reputation with *Axel's Castle*, a study of exactly the writers Trilling considered canonical (Yeats, Eliot, Joyce, and Proust, to whom Wilson added Stein and Valéry). Trilling's own reputation, by contrast, was made with a biographical study of Matthew Arnold—a writer whom he recognized, in the 1930s, was as unfashionable as possible.

One reason why Trilling did not write about the modernists is, perhaps, because Wilson and so many others did. If the 1930s and '40s were what Randall Jarrell called "The Age of Criticism" (the title of an essay published, naturally, in *Partisan Review*), this was mainly because modernist literature seemed to require so much explication. On several occasions, Jarrell wrote, he asked people if they had read Eliot's poem "Gerontion" and received a reply along the lines of, "Well, not really—I've *read* it, but I've never read a thorough analysis of it." The prestige of certain modernist and proto-modernist writers was so great, he complains, that no one seemed to read anything else. At "literary parties," he writes, "if you wanted to talk about *Ulysses* or *The Castle* or *The Brothers Karamazov* or *The Great Gatsby. . . .* Important books—you were at the right place." But if you tried to bring up anything else—and Jarrell names more than a dozen other works by everyone from Balzac to Mark Twain—"you couldn't expect a very ready knowledge or sympathy."

Yet as Jarrell himself once remarked, "The people who live in a Golden Age usually go around complaining how yellow everything looks." And what he attacked as a trendy narrowness can appear, from the vantage point of our own, radically decentered literary culture, like an enviable form of consensus. One reason why Trilling found it so useful to use the first person plural is that it reflected (and enforced) an agreement among serious readers about which books and writers it was necessary to know. That agreement made possible critical discussions of a complexity and intensity that are hard to recapture now, when a critic can never assume that any of her concerns or allusions will automatically be shared by her audience. For Trilling, it was unnecessary to explicate Eliot or Mann, or to argue for their importance; he could resort to listing the modernists, because he could assume that his readers were as "intimate" with them as he was.

There is also a sense, however, in which Trilling's evasion of the modernists was a deliberate tactical maneuver. For his task as a critic was not to expound modernism but to put it into question—more precisely, to put into question the assumptions and beliefs of readers like himself, whose admiration of writers like Yeats and Lawrence went along with a principled distrust of many of the things Yeats and Lawrence praised. In fact, the best way to describe Trilling's uniqueness as a critic is to say that he was always less concerned with writers than with readers, less interested in the way novels work than in the way we put them to work in our own lives. As he puts it, "my own interests lead me to see literary situations as cultural situations, and cultural situations as great elaborate fights about moral issues, and moral issues as having something to do with gratuitously chosen images of personal being, and images of personal being as having something to do with literary style."

This description of his own method comes from the essay in which Trilling offered his most comprehensive diagnosis of the modern "literary situation": "On the Teaching of Modern Literature," from *Beyond Culture*. Here, if anywhere, one might expect to find Trilling reflecting on the modernist classics, since he starts out by mentioning that all the familiar names—"Yeats and Eliot . . . Proust and Kafka . . . Lawrence, Mann and Gide"—were on the syllabus of the course on modern literature that he taught at Columbia. Yet even as he describes the course, Trilling dwells on his deep reluctance to teach these writers, or even to see them taught in the university at all. "Up to a few years ago," he writes in this 1961 essay, Columbia English courses went no further than the late nineteenth century, and he approved of this reticence. Only when the students demanded a course on twentieth-century literature did the department consent to offer one, and even then Trilling describes this as a capitulation, accompanied by "a certain mean-spirited, last-ditch vindictiveness."

The reason Trilling is so unwilling to teach the modernists is closely related to the reason why he declined to write about them. It is not, of course, that he was uninterested in them, but that he was too interested, too personally involved, to treat them simply as items on a syllabus. In fact, he goes on to argue, this is precisely what makes modern literature modern (the original title of the essay was "On the Modern Element in Modern Literature"): that it is impossible to read or talk about it without being personally implicated, even exposed.

This "extravagant personal force of modern literature," as Trilling describes it, is a product of its extravagant hostility to conventional patterns of civilized life. "No literature has ever been so shockingly personal as that of our time," Trilling writes. "It asks every question that is forbidden in polite society. It asks us if we are content with our marriages, with our family lives, with our professional lives, with our friends." Trilling does not give many examples, but he does not need to; open any page of the authors he mentions, and the questions are impossible to avoid. They are there in "The Waste Land":

> *Datta*: what have we given?
> My friend, blood shaking my heart
> The awful daring of a moment's surrender
> Which an age of prudence can never retract
> By this, and this only, we have existed
> Which is not to be found in our obituaries
> Or in memories draped by the beneficent spider
> Or under seals broken by the lean solicitor
> In our empty rooms

And they are there, more belligerently put, in Lawrence's "How Beastly the Bourgeois Is":

How beastly the bourgeois is
especially the male of the species—

Nicely groomed, like a mushroom
standing there so sleek and erect and eyeable—
and like a fungus, living on the remains of a bygone life
sucking his life out of the dead leaves of greater life
than his own.

And even so, he's stale, he's been there too long.
Touch him, and you'll find he's all gone inside
just like an old mushroom, all wormy inside, and hollow
under a smooth skin and an upright appearance.

"How, except with the implication of personal judgment, does one say to students that Gide is perfectly accurate in his representation of the awful boredom and slow corruption of respectable life?" Trilling asks, and the question is easily extended. How can you teach Eliot's lines about daring and prudence without talking about the kind of experiences that are not to be found in your obituary—or, most of the time, in your lecture notes? How can you confirm or deny Lawrence's indictment of the bourgeois without explaining whether you yourself are stale and all gone inside?

The only alternative to such personal testimony, Trilling writes, is to swathe these bomb-like books in abstractions, so that the student never feels their explosive force at all. He mocks this approach by imagining an exam question: "Compare Yeats, Gide, Lawrence, and Eliot in the use which they make of the theme of sexuality to criticize the deficiencies of modern culture . . . Time: one hour." Yet of course questions like this are asked on exams all the time, including Trilling's own exams, because in the classroom there is no way to measure the personal transformation wrought by a work of literature. That is why "when modern literature is brought into the classroom, the subject being taught is betrayed by the pedagogy of the subject."

The way Trilling solved this problem as a teacher sheds light on the way he approached it as a critic. In "On the Teaching of Modern Literature," as in his criticism as a whole, Trilling says almost nothing about the masterpieces of modernism that presumably formed the core of his syllabus. Instead, he chooses to discuss a number of short texts that he selected to give students a sense of the "background" of modernism, "older books [that] might seem to fall into a line the direction of which pointed to our literature." Most of these are not even literary, in the narrow sense of fiction and poetry, but works of anthropology, psychology, and philosophy. In this way, Trilling sketches a certain interpretation of modernism, and of the whole intellectual culture of the modern period, which indirectly but powerfully expresses his own sense of that culture's terrible, antinomian force.

The earliest book on Trilling's syllabus is *Rameau's Nephew,* a dialogue written in the 1760s by the *philosophe* and Encyclo-pedist Denis Diderot. At first glance, this might look like a period piece, stuffed as it is with snide remarks about a host of now-forgotten Parisian society figures. These insults come from the lips of Rameau, a nephew and namesake of the great com-poser, whom we see buttonholing Diderot at a cafe and pouring out a stream of abuse and complaint—about corrupt officials, actresses who are really courtesans, fraudulent music teachers, his miserly uncle, and on and on. One intention of the work, certainly, is to expose the vices of the *ancien régime*: "Virtue is praised, but hated. People run away from it, for it is ice-cold and in this world you must keep your feet warm," says Rameau.

But if this were all Diderot had to say, the dialogue would not have exerted such a powerful influence on everyone from Goethe, who translated it into German, to Hegel, who wrote about it in the *Phenomenology of Spirit,* to Marx and Freud, both of whom admired it greatly. What makes it, in Trilling's words, "peculiarly relevant to the line taken by the ethical explorations of modern literature" is the way Diderot makes Rameau at once morally appalling and hugely charismatic. Di-derot achieves this effect in part thanks to the dialogue struc-ture, which allows him to split his intelligence between the character bearing his own name—the dialogue's "Moi"—and Rameau, its "Lui." Whenever Diderot speaks as "Moi," he is rational, moderate, and virtuous: "Sometimes a gay party with my friends, even if it is a little rowdy, is not displeasing to me. But I must confess that I find it infinitely sweeter to succor the unfortunate, to disentangle a bad business, to give helpful advice, to read a pleasant book."

Yet this sort of right-mindedness looks pale next to the pyrotechnical vice of Rameau—a man so degraded that he has just lost his sinecure as a nobleman's jester and flatterer, because he made a joke too coarse even for a jester to get away with. "I am an ignoramus, a fool, a lunatic, a lazy, impudent, greedy good-for-nothing," he announces with perverse pride. But what makes Rameau more than a mere boor is the fact that he is also a thwarted artist—a musician who, unable to compose a masterpiece like his famous uncle, pours his genius into wild, mocking and self-mocking impersonations and pantomimes. His vice is his revenge on society and on himself, and this gives it an undeniable impressiveness. At one point, when Rameau is acting out a scene involving a nobleman's pimp and the girl he is trying to seduce, Diderot writes: "I hardly knew whether to burst with laughter or indignation. I was in pain: a dozen times laughter kept anger down; a dozen times my deepening anger had to end in a shout of laughter. I was overcome by so much cunning and baseness, by notions so exact and at the same time so false, by so complete a perversion of feeling, by such turpitude and such frankness, both equally uncommon."

What Diderot created, Trilling writes, was the first anti-hero:

a figure who, by refusing to apologize for his viciousness, seems to make vice a kind of distinction, and forces us to confront the evil in our own nature. Returning to the dialogue in his last book, *Sincerity and Authenticity,* Trilling writes that its "entrancing power" comes from the way it suggests "that moral judgment is not ultimate, that man's nature and destiny are not wholly comprehended within the narrow space between virtue and vice." The Nephew is the first in the line of social outcasts and brilliant mockers who are the heroes of so much modern fiction, from Dostoevsky's Underground Man to Camus's Stranger.

Notes from Underground, in fact, is one of the works of fiction on Trilling's syllabus, along with Conrad's *Heart of Darkness* and Mann's *Death in Venice.* One attraction of these books for Trilling the professor was surely pragmatic—they are short, and so easier to assign than, say, *The Brothers Karamazov* and *The Magic Mountain.* But they also help to sharpen Trilling's sense of modern literature's fascination with evil. The characters at the center of these works are civilized, responsible men— Mann's Aschenbach is a sternly disciplined and productive writer, much like Mann himself, while Conrad's Kurtz, Trilling writes, "is a progressive and a liberal . . . the highly respected representative of a society which would have us believe it is benign."

Yet the fates of these men suggest that civilization is no

match for the cruelty, lust, and violence that make up our secret, truest selves. The Heart of Darkness is, famously, not just the Congo, but Kurtz's own heart: the liberal ends up as a genocidal, cannibalistic man-god, ruling savagely over a remote tribe. And Aschenbach stays in plague-ridden Venice, guaranteeing his own death, because his desire for the young boy Tadzio is stronger than his desire for survival. Trilling alludes to, but doesn't quote, the passage in *Death in Venice* where Aschenbach dreams of a primitive orgy:

> His senses reeled in the steam of panting bodies, the acrid stench from the goats, the odor as of stagnant waters—and another, too familiar smell—of wounds, uncleanness, and disease. His heart throbbed to the drums, his brain reeled, a blind rage seized him, a whirling lust, he craved with all his soul to join the ring that formed about the obscene symbol of the godhead. . . . Yes, it was he who was flinging himself upon the animals, who bit and tore and swallowed smoking gobbets of flesh—while on the trampled moss there now began the rites in honor of the god, an orgy of promiscuous embraces—and in his very soul he tasted the bestial degradation of his fall.

If the reversion to savagery were simply a "fall," however, it would not pose such a profound challenge. The knowledge that human beings, even the best, are capable of sin is not a modern discovery. What is distinctive in modern literature is the idea that what we call evil is actually good: that the primal is superior to the civilized, passion superior to reason. As Trilling

writes in "The Fate of Pleasure," "Whenever in modern literature we find violence, whether of represented act or of expression, and an insistence upon the sordid and the disgusting, and
an insult offered to the prevailing morality or habit of life, we
may assume that we are in the presence of the intention to
destroy specious good." The nonfiction works that Trilling includes on his syllabus all give their sanction to this antinomian
belief. They create an intellectual climate in which the intellect
itself can be seen as humanity's great burden and enemy.

Thus the orgy described by Mann, Trilling points out, is
unmistakably an evocation of the rites of Dionysus as described
by Nietzsche in *The Birth of Tragedy,* one of the philosophical
works on Trilling's syllabus. Ostensibly, Nietzsche's argument is
that Greek tragedy, which he considers the highest art form ever
created, was the result of a union between Apollo—the principle
of vision, form, and measure—and Dionysus—the principle
of music, terror, and ecstasy. But while both principles are necessary for great art, there can be no mistaking that the rhetorical
force of Nietzsche's essay is all with Dionysus: "under the influence of the narcotic draught . . . or with the potent coming of
spring that penetrates all nature, these Dionysian emotions
awake, and as they grow in intensity everything subjective van-
ishes into complete self-forgetfulness. . . . Just as the animals
now talk, and the earth yields milk and honey, supernatural
sounds emanate from him, too: he feels himself a god, he him-

self now walks about enchanted, in ecstasy, like the gods he saw walking in his dream." Compared to this kind of primal energy, what good is the conventional morality of an Aschenbach, a Kurtz, a Diderot? They seem like what Nietzsche calls "poor wretches [who] have no idea how corpselike and ghostly their own 'healthy-mindedness' looks when the glowing life of the Dionysian revelers roars past them."

What is most troubling to Trilling, however, is to find Sigmund Freud coming to the same dark conclusion. Freud meant at least as much to Trilling as any novelist or poet. "The pleasure I have in listening to Freud," he wrote, "I find very difficult to distinguish from the pleasure which is involved in responding to a satisfactory work of art." He devoted several essays to Freud, and while these express some reservations about the Freudian system—in particular, its understanding of the purpose of art and the psychology of the artist—Trilling never stopped praising what he called "the quality of grim poetry" in Freud's work, "its ultimate tragic courage." This is the courage to recognize that human existence is tragic, that our nature is made for unhappiness, and to persevere despite this in the compensatory work of civilization—of which Freud's own research was an inspiring example.

Yet in *Civilization and Its Discontents,* chronologically the last work on Trilling's syllabus, even Freud begins to question whether, as Trilling puts it, "we want to *accept* civilization."

After a lifetime devoted to the healthy mind—if not exactly to what Nietzsche called "healthy-mindedness"—Freud asks, in this 1929 essay, whether life in modern society makes true health impossible. Ever since the first human beings began to live in groups, his argument runs, they have had to learn to repress their sexual and aggressive instincts: "It is impossible to overlook the extent to which civilization is built upon a renunciation of instinct." But while Freud places a high value on the fruits of renunciation, he also recognizes that it is an extremely painful process, because "the feeling of happiness derived from the satisfaction of a wild instinctual impulse untamed by the ego is incomparably more intense than that derived from sating an instinct that has been tamed" (a sentiment that Aschenbach, for one, would certainly share).

What, then, if modern Western civilization, with all its social disciplines and economic demands and religious prohibitions, has reached a point of diminishing returns? What if it demands more sacrifice of libido and aggression than the individual can afford? "The sexual life of civilized man is . . . severely impaired," Freud writes, even wondering if sexuality is "in the process of involution as a function, just as our teeth and hair seem to be as organs. One is probably justified in assuming that its importance as a source of feelings of happiness . . . has sensibly diminished." If things have reached this pass, he asks, "May we not be justified in reaching the diagnosis that . . . some civilizations, or some epochs of civilization—possibly the whole of mankind—have become 'neurotic'?" And if civilization is making man sick, wouldn't he do best to get rid of it?

To Trilling, this is the central question of modern literature, the one that is asked in various ways by everyone from Diderot to Lawrence. And because this critique of civilization is so profound and total, every reader becomes its target: its existential demands can be answered only in the first person. Modern writers insist that we question ourselves, and Trilling believed that Goethe posed the essential modern question when he asked, "But is this really true—is it true for me?" In this sense, Trilling's reluctance to write about or teach the modernist literature that meant most to him is exemplary. He is put at a loss by these books, and his embarrassment shows that reading seriously, even for a reader as masterful as Trilling, involves resistance as well as acquiescence to the author's will.

6

"howl"
and the
visionary
gleam

If Wordsworth, for Trilling, represents the wisdom of passiveness, then the poet who best
represents the modern desire
for rebellion and unmasking,
for the transvaluation of social
and aesthetic values, is William
Blake. Blake's "Proverbs of Hell"
is the classic example, in English
literature, of "insult offered to
the prevailing morality" in the
name of a more primal truth:

> The road of excess leads to the
>   palace of wisdom.
> If the fool would persist in his
>   folly he would become wise.
> The soul of sweet delight can
>   never be defiled.
> Sooner murder an infant in its
>   cradle than nurse unacted
>   desires.

This antinomianism, Trilling says in "Wordsworth and the Rabbis," is what makes Blake typical of "the quality of the militancy of most modern writers." "Nothing is better established in our literary life than the knowledge that the tigers of wrath are to be preferred to the horses of instruction, a striking remark which is indeed sometimes very true, although not always," he says of Blake's famous aphorism. Trilling never devoted a full essay to Blake, but he mentions him on several occasions as a tutelary genius of the modern age—"the outraged spirit of William Blake, in whose existence we all now participate." Trilling considered him a particularly important influence on the counterculture of the 1960s: "American undergraduates seem to be ever more alienated from the general body of English literature, but they had for some time made an exception of William Blake, pledging him their unquestioning allegiance, and in 1968, when the large majority of the students at my university were either committed to or acquiescent in its disruption, they found him uniquely relevant to their spiritual aspirations."

In fact, by a strangely ironic chance, Trilling himself was a mentor to the poet who did most to transmit Blake's legacy to the 1960s. In 1944, as a seventeen-year-old freshman, Allen Ginsberg signed up for Trilling's course on the Great Books at Columbia, and soon became close to his professor. During the war years, the college was overloaded with officer training candidates, most of whom had no real interest in Trilling's thoughts on the Great Books; in Ginsberg, on the other hand, he found a student who was already an aspiring writer. Ginsberg also later suggested that "I was probably closest to Trilling because we were both Jewish and he sort of empathized with me."

Ginsberg sorely tested the limits of that empathy. He visited Trilling at home and sent him long letters; he even showed Trilling the poems he was writing, which he was afraid to do with his father, Louis Ginsberg, who wrote conventional magazine verse. Ginsberg told Trilling that "my father and I differ so violently on poetic method that I hesitate to ask him for advice and criticism"; in other words, he was asking Trilling to serve in his father's place. But even this wasn't enough, and in 1947, he sent Trilling a letter saying that he was trying to write "fully and directly enough to break down—what is it? Our mutual distrust."

Trilling, as might be expected, tried to hold this presumptuous student at arm's length, to preserve some of the teacher-student hierarchy. He replied to Ginsberg's letter this way:

> In itself it is really quite simple: it is that I think our relationship is not intended to be the kind you assume in your letter. Its right condition is set by the original connection between us, that of student and teacher, and by the difference in our ages. . . . If you present your life to me in the manner that you have done, I am willing to receive seriously and affectionately what you tell me, but I can do

that only as your teacher and older friend; it would be impossible and pointless for me to reciprocate in anything approaching kind.

But being Ginsberg's mentor entailed a constant violation of the usual boundaries. The most striking example came when Ginsberg was hauled up before the dean of Columbia for an infraction that, today, seems quite ludicrous. In the dust on his dorm-room window, he had traced the messages "Butler has no balls" (a reference to the university's president, Nicholas Murray Butler) and "Fuck the Jews," accompanied by drawings of a penis and a skull. At the time, however, neither the profanity nor the disrespect for authority was taken lightly, and when the slogans were discovered, Ginsberg was made to withdraw from school for a year. The punishment might have been worse if Trilling had not intervened on his student's behalf. As Diana Trilling recalled years later in "The Other Night at Columbia," her mordant account of a Beat poetry reading:

> the words were too shocking for the Dean of students to speak, so he had written them on a piece of paper which he pushed across the desk to my husband: "Fuck the Jews." Even the part of Lionel that wanted to laugh couldn't; it was too hard for the Dean to have to transmit this message to a Jewish professor—this was still in the forties when being a Jew in the university was not yet what it is today. "But he's a Jew himself," said the Dean. "Can you understand his writing a thing like that?" Yes, Lionel could understand; but he couldn't explain it to the Dean. And anyway, he

knew that to appreciate why Ginsberg had traced this particular legend on the window required more than an understanding of Jewish self-hatred.

Ginsberg always denied that "self-hatred" had anything to do with it. In fact, he claimed, he had been trying in a convoluted way to provoke his Irish chambermaid, whom he suspected of not cleaning his room properly because *she* was anti-Semitic. In any case, Trilling did defend Ginsberg from the Dean; and he defended him again in 1949, in a more serious situation, when Ginsberg had already left Columbia. This was when he got arrested for being the accomplice of a thief named Herbert Huncke, one of the low-lifes he glamorized as an example of Beat alienation. This time it was Ginsberg's father who turned to Trilling for help, writing to him: "ever since Allen entered college, your name has been a household word with us. He has read, and we have discussed, your articles (in *The Partisan Review, Kenyon Review,* etc.) Allen looks up to you with something of veneration." Trilling helped convince the police to send Ginsberg to a mental hospital rather than to jail; and it was during his year at the New York State Psychiatric Institute that he met Carl Solomon, the saintly psychotic who was the addressee of "Howl." In this strange, roundabout way, Trilling made "Howl" possible.

In "The Other Night at Columbia," Diana Trilling records

her extreme impatience with Ginsberg's behavior, and with her husband's solicitude:

> Allen Ginsberg had been a student of my husband's and I had heard about him much more than I usually hear of students for the simple reason that he got into a great deal of trouble which involved his instructors, and had to be rescued and revived and restored; eventually he even had to be kept out of jail. Of course there was always the question, should this young man be rescued, should he be restored? There was even the question, shouldn't he go to jail? We argued about it some at home but the discussion, I'm afraid, was academic, despite my old resistance to the idea that people like Ginsberg had the right to ask and receive preferential treatment just because they read Rimbaud and Gide and undertook to be writers themselves. . . . Why should I not . . . defend the expectation that a student at Columbia, even a poet, would do his work, submit it to his teachers through the normal channels of classroom communication, stay out of jail, and, if things went right, graduate, start publishing, be reviewed, and see what developed, whether he was a success or failure?

But Lionel Trilling, clearly, could not share this uncomplicated view of literature as a career in which you progress by regular steps, like a junior executive racking up promotions. On the contrary, he had to acknowledge that Ginsberg's personal and literary rebellion against convention was in the authentic tradition of modernism. Wasn't there an affinity between Ginsberg's glamorization of thieves and Babel's glamorization of Cossacks, those seductive lawbreakers? Wasn't Ginsberg's experimentation with sex and drugs comparable to that of Baudelaire and Rimbaud? Even if Ginsberg was, perhaps, mad, wasn't it a central principle of modern literature that madness and genius were allied? "The artist sees as insane the 'normal' and 'healthy' ways of established society," Trilling wrote in "Art and Neurosis," "while aberration and illness appear as spiritual and moral health if only because they controvert the ways of respectable society." Trilling did not endorse this view—the essay as a whole is an attack on "the myth of the sick artist"—but he could not deny that it found support from canonical writers.

Blake, for instance, figured centrally in Ginsberg's explorations of the limits of sanity. In 1948, while he was finishing his last credits before graduating Columbia, he had a series of disturbing but exhilarating visionary experiences. The most significant of these came one day when he was masturbating, and at the moment of orgasm heard what he knew to be the voice of William Blake reciting "Ah, Sunflower":

> Ah, Sunflower, weary of time,
> Who countest the steps of the sun;
> Seeking after that sweet golden clime
> Where the traveller's journey is done;
>
> Where the Youth pined away with desire,
> And the pale virgin shrouded in snow,
> Arise from their graves, and aspire
> Where my Sunflower wishes to go!

It was a fitting poem to hear in those particular circumstances: Blake writes about embracing sex and desire, about escaping the pale, pining, repressed earth for the blazing, golden sun. But sex, in Blake, is not just sex. It is bliss and holiness, it is the road to universal communion. And for a moment, in the summer of his twenty-first year, Ginsberg believed that he had experienced the universal oneness that is the goal of mystics in every religious tradition. "These experiences," he later said, "because of their absolute and eternal nature [became] . . . the keystone and reference point for all of my thought—a North Star for life; much as Dante says, Incipit Vita Nuova."

Seven years later, when Ginsberg finally found a way to translate this exaltation into verse, he produced "Howl." It is a Blakean poem through and through, whose epigraph might be "everything that lives is holy." Or, as Ginsberg puts it:

> Holy! Holy! Holy! Holy! Holy! Holy! Holy! Holy! Holy! Holy!
>   Holy! Holy! Holy!
>   Holy! Holy!
> The world is holy! The soul is holy! The skin is holy! The nose is
>   holy! The tongue
>   and cock and hand and asshole holy!
> Everything is holy! Everybody's holy! Everywhere is holy!
>   Everyday is in eternity!
>   Everyman's an angel!
> The bum's as holy as the seraphim! The madman is holy as you
>   my soul are holy!

Ginsberg needs those fifteen repetitions of "Holy," just as he needs words like cock and asshole, because like all mystics he knows how unwilling people are to hear and believe his message. It is the same reason why he sometimes took his clothes off at his poetry readings, and was once photographed naked. Society needs to be shocked out of its respectable, defensive habits, forced to acknowledge that there is no shame in nakedness and sex, or for that matter in poverty and suffering. As Ginsberg wrote in his most explicit homage to Blake, "Sunflower Sutra": "We're not our skin of grime, we're not our dread bleak dusty imageless locomotive, we're all golden sunflowers inside, blessed by our own seed & hairy naked accomplishment-bodies growing into mad black formal sunflowers in the sunset."

In 1956, Ginsberg sent Trilling a copy of the book of "Howl" that had just been published by City Lights in San Francisco. He would have been justified in hoping for an explosive reaction, for at many points, "Howl" reads like an attack on Columbia and its intellectual culture, of which Trilling was the living symbol. The first strophes of the poem mention "negro streets," invoking the Harlem neighborhood next to Columbia's Morningside Heights campus. The poem's "angelheaded hipsters" are specifically cast as students who rebel against "universities" and "academies." The faculty, on the other hand, are "scholars of war"—a shorthand attack on the Cold War alliance of anti-Communists in government and academia, of which Trilling was again a prominent example. There is even, perhaps, an allusion to Ginsberg's notorious dorm-room graffiti when he writes about "obscene odes on the window of the skull"—after all, his obscene writing on the dust of his window was accompanied by a skull.

One can imagine his disappointment, then, when Trilling wrote back saying that he found the poem "dull." This seems an unlikely verdict on a poem that, whatever its flaws, can hardly be called boring. But for a reader like Trilling, who spent his whole career wrestling with the transgressions of the moderns, Ginsberg's *dérèglement de tous les sens* could not be the explosive discovery it would become for a generation of American readers. "As to the doctrinal element of the poems," he explained, "apart from the fact that I of course reject it, it seems to me that I heard it very long ago and that you give it to me in all its orthodoxy, with nothing new added." The more urgently Ginsberg strove to provoke, the more coolly Trilling responded with condescension—a kind of rebuke also evident in Diana Trilling's essay, where she compares the Beats and their followers to children in a progressive kindergarten.

There is, however, something a little too insistent about Trilling's "of course." It was by no means simple or unambiguous for Trilling, who felt so strongly the charm of Di Grasso's leap, to keep his own feet planted sensibly on the ground. "I venture to say," he confided in "On the Teaching of Modern Literature," "that the idea of losing oneself to the point of self-destruction, of surrendering oneself to experience without regard to self-interest or conventional morality, of escaping wholly from the societal bonds, is an 'element' somewhere in the mind of every modern person who dares to think of what Arnold in his un-affected Victorian way called 'the fulness of spiritual perfection.'" Trilling did believe, as he told Ginsberg, that a mature and ethical disillusionment was superior to a naïve intoxication with transcendence; but it was a belief he embraced with effort, and never unreservedly.

He can be heard arguing it with himself in his essay on Wordsworth's Immortality Ode, where he once again turns to Wordsworth as a representative of wisdom, and a counter-weight to the passion of a Blake. This essay, included in *The Liberal Imagination*, was written in 1941, when Trilling was thirty-five—just the age of Dante's *mezzo del cammin di nostra vita*, the "middle of the journey" which he was to invoke in the title of his novel. The Immortality Ode was an ideal subject for Trilling at such a turning point, since it is the rare modern poem in which aging is affirmed and embraced. It is much more common, in modern literature, for aging to be experienced as a degradation and an insult, as it was for Yeats ("An aged man is but a paltry thing, / A tattered coat upon a stick"). It has always seemed fatefully appropriate that the

English Romantic poets mostly died young, before their passion and aspiration could be humbled in this way.

Wordsworth, of course, was the great exception—the youthful Romantic who lived to a patriarchal age, and died full of honors. Yet Wordsworth, too, can be taken to prove the incompatibility of poetic passion with middle age. Almost all his great poems were written by the age of forty, and his later work, though voluminous, has become a byword for tedium. This fact, Trilling complains, has led critics to read the Immortality Ode, which Wordsworth wrote at thirty-two, as "a dirge sung over departing powers." "Whither is fled the visionary gleam? / Where is it now, the glory and the dream?" the poet asks. Readers have not unreasonably felt that this was a "conscious farewell to art," Trilling writes, since they take "for granted that the visionary gleam, the glory and the dream, are Wordsworth's name for the power by which he made poetry."

Trilling's extended close reading of the poem—the only such reading he ever published—powerfully refutes this view. Rather, he argues, what Wordsworth is really writing about, under the name of "the visionary gleam," is not a specifically poetic power, but a universal human experience, "a period common to the development of everyone." This is the child's intuition of being at one with the universe—what Freud called the "oceanic" sensation, of which adult religious emotions are the after-echoes. Trilling quotes *Civilization and Its Discontents:* "Originally the ego includes everything, later it detaches from itself the outside world. The ego-feeling we are aware of now is thus only a shrunken vestige of a more extensive feeling—a feeling which embraced the universe and expressed an inseparable connection of the ego with the external world." It is in this Freudian sense, Trilling suggests, that we should read Wordsworth's lament, "But yet I know, where'er I go, / That there hath past away a glory from the earth."

Trilling follows Freud in believing strongly that the loss of this glory is a necessary and desirable step on the path to maturity—what Wordsworth calls "the philosophic mind," what Trilling calls "the sense of reality." It is natural to regret childish illusions, but it would be perverse to prolong them, since "we fulfill ourselves by choosing what is painful and difficult and necessary, and we develop by moving toward death." This affirmation of tragic necessity is what Trilling finds in the last section of the Immortality Ode, where Wordsworth declares that the loss of the "gleam" has brought with it the gain of other powers and perceptions: "The Clouds that gather round the setting sun / Do take a sober colouring from an eye / That hath kept watch o'er man's mortality." It follows that the philosophic mind should be able to produce a new kind of poetry, different from the "visionary" art of youth, but not necessarily less powerful. For this reason, Trilling insists, the Ode is "so little a dirge sung over departing powers, that it is actually the very opposite—it is a welcome of new powers and a dedication to a new poetic subject."

This is a very convincing reading of the Ode, and consonant with the ideas about growth and perception that Wordsworth explores in many other works, from "Tintern Abbey" to "The Prelude." But Trilling grows significantly less confident when addressing what is, after all, the crucial question: if maturity brings new poetic powers, why did these powers not allow Wordsworth to write great poetry in the second half of his life? In the last pages of the essay, Trilling offers several evasive responses to this question, before settling on a principled agnosticism: "in our present state of knowledge, we cannot begin to furnish" an explanation of the growth or waning of poetic powers.

What Trilling does not want to countenance is the possibility that his reading of the Ode, as a welcome to maturity and reality, and the traditional reading, which sees it as a farewell to genius, are complementary—that they imply one another. For this would be to say that Wordsworth's "philosophic mind" was what killed his poetry, that too keen a "sense of reality" is simply incompatible with art. This is, of course, yet another way of stating the same opposition that Trilling encounters so often in his criticism—between genius and justice.

No wonder, then, that Trilling responded so strictly and summarily to "Howl." The poem's whole force lies in its insistence that youth and age, soul and mind, are indeed bitter enemies: "Moloch whose name is the Mind" feeds on the vital forces of Ginsberg's wrecked generation. The poem asserts the very incompatibility that Trilling tried hard, in his essay on "The Immortality Ode" and elsewhere, to deny. More, Ginsberg was implicitly casting himself as the representative of genius—lawless, vital, sexual, young—which meant putting Trilling in the role of justice—wise, well-adjusted, but uncreative. In 1955, just after writing "Howl," Ginsberg raged in his journal: "Trilling doesn't think the individual is important. Just his Wisdom. As if his Wisdom could be separated from the mistakes juices & privacies of his life. He's rejected himself." The critic's coolness toward such a view is understandable.

But it was not wholly candid. One of the strangest things about Trilling's relationship with Ginsberg is the way that it seems to raise, in real life, questions that he had already addressed through the medium of fiction, in his 1943 short story "Of This Time, Of That Place." This story, the best of the few Trilling published, was completed before he met Ginsberg; yet the relationship between Joseph Howe, the story's mild-mannered poet-professor, and Ferdinand Tertan, a brilliantly mad student, is uncannily suggestive of his own relationship with Ginsberg. This is another sign of how Trilling, in a way more characteristic of creative writers than critics, seemed to shape his life to suit the obsessions of his work, and vice versa.

In the story, however, Trilling could allow himself more sympathy with transgression and even madness than he would in reality. From the beginning, Howe is shown to be as uneasy in combining the roles of pedagogue and creative writer as Trilling himself. He has just published his third book of poems, which we learn has been rebuked by a critic for being too "esoteric"; clearly Howe is enough of a modernist and an aesthete to take pride in such attacks. Yet he is also enough of a bourgeois and a pedagogue to take pleasure in wearing a doctoral gown and mortarboard in the college Convocation—what Trilling calls "the weighty and absurd symbols" of his profession.

The tension between these roles comes into the open when Tertan, a new student, presents himself in class and immediately proposes a kind of conspiracy of genius with Howe—just the kind of illegitimate intimacy Ginsberg sought with Trilling. "Some professors are pedants. They are dryasdusts. However, some professors are free souls and creative spirits. Kant, Hegel, and Nietzsche were all professors. It is my opinion that you occupy the second category," Tertan proclaims, hitting instinctively on Howe's greatest fear—that he cannot be both a professor and a free soul.

This fear the story finally confirms, when Howe comes to the realization that Tertan is not just eccentric but actually insane. He knows the right thing to do is to hand the matter over to the Dean, which will result in Tertan being expelled. But when he does this, Howe is plagued by guilt, by his sense that he should have remained loyal to the "creative spirit" that he and Tertan share. Certainly Howe infinitely prefers Tertan to another student, Blackburn, who is ruthlessly ambitious and unethical, worldly in the worst sense. Tertan's madness seems more sane to Howe than Blackburn's sanity—precisely the kind of inversion that Ginsberg makes in "Howl."

The heart of the story can be found in a phrase Trilling uses early on, when Howe is about to enter his classroom and has a momentary fear of "the lawful seizure of power he was about to make." At the same time that Trilling understands the need for mature authority, he also feels that it is somehow illegitimate for himself to be the one wielding that authority. He has too much sympathy for disorder to be simply a spokesman for order; yet he is too sane to pretend to be mad, and too adult to pretend to be young. (Writing about his early mentor Elliot Cohen, Trilling praised him because he "never played the game of being young.") Only a writer who allowed himself to be inhabited by both sides of this dialectic could have produced a criticism at once so magisterial and so daringly exposed.

7

the affirming self

If modern literature is, as Trilling argues, a literature of aggression, of critique and contempt, then the only way to fully experience it is to be threatened by it. Any purely formalist approach to literature is simply an evasion of this threat—like praising the design of a revolver that is being pointed at your head. "Structures of words [the modernists] may indeed have created," he writes in "On the Teaching of Modern Literature," "but these structures were not pyramids or triumphal arches, they were manifestly contrived to be not static and commemorative but mobile and aggressive, and one does not describe a quinqui-reme or a howitzer without estimating how much *damage* it can do."

For this reason, the only way to accept modern literature is to resist it—to be its worthy antagonist. Trilling even writes with wry admiration about those of his students who are frankly disgusted and bewildered by the books he assigns them: "I find that I am sometimes moved to give them a queer respect, as if they had stood up and said what in fact they don't have the wit to stand up and say: 'Why do you harry us? Leave us alone.'" It is these students, whose conventionality or religious belief or sheltered upbringing have left them susceptible to the scandal of modernism, who "make ready the way for 'the good and the beautiful' about which low-minded doubts have been raised in this course, that 'good and beautiful' which we do not possess and don't want to possess but which we know justifies our lives."

Such students may or may not really exist, but they occupy an important place in Trilling's critical imagination. They represent the possibility that there are still, even in the twentieth century, people who affirm the good and the beautiful in the way that the German Romantic writer Friedrich Schiller, in his classic essay "On Naïve and Sentimental Poetry," called naïve: "a heart full of innocence and truth, which out of inner greatness disdains the help of art." Such innocents continue to cherish an uncomplicated ideal of human happiness, the very ideal that modern literature devotes itself to undermining. In *Sincerity and Authenticity,* Trilling describes this "norm of life" as one of "order, peace, honor, and beauty"—or, in words he quotes from *The Tempest,* "Honor, riches, marriage blessing, / Long continuance and increasing." "It has to do," he elaborates, "with good harvests and full barns and . . . affluent decorum": the kind of material prosperity we strive for in our actual lives, but which we find boring and philistine when it comes to literature.

In a sense, Trilling wants philistine readers to exist precisely because, without them, the attacking force of modernism can find no target. Yet Trilling himself, whose mind was formed by modernism, can never be that kind of naïve reader. This is clear even, or especially, in the rare moments when he experiments with condemning modern literature on moral grounds. In a diary entry of 1948, he writes: "Nowadays, we are all Aristotelians in our aesthetics and we are certain that the theory of art that Plato proposes in *The Republic* is false and naïve. Yet there is truth in the belief that we become assimilated to the literal contents of the art we contemplate. . . . It is possible that our contemplation of cruelty will not make us humane but cruel; that the reiteration of the badness of our spiritual condition will make us consent to it."

The Platonic theory of art to which Trilling refers is laid out in Book III of *The Republic,* where Socrates and Adeimantus discuss whether the ideal city will permit poetry to be taught and recited. They decide that it will not, since—as Socrates shows with numerous citations from Homer—the poets represent the gods as doing all kinds of ignoble things, which will lead citizens astray if they try to emulate them. The assumption that people naturally imitate the things they hear about in poetry is at the core of Plato's doctrine, and it justifies his insistence that "some tales are to be told, and others are not to be told to our disciples from their youth upwards, if we mean them to honor the gods and their parents, and to value friendship with one another."

In the privacy of his diary, Trilling experiments with the possibility of endorsing this view; but of course, he finally can't help sharing the common modern opinion, that it is "false and naïve." After all, Trilling himself was shaped by modern literature, with all its subversions and transgressions, yet his own life was quite conventional and respectable. Indeed, he was widely admired as a teacher, in which role he was responsible for introducing young people to Kurtz's cannibalism and Aschenbach's pederasty. If he really believed that "we become assimilated to the literal contents of the art we contemplate," he would have to condemn himself as a corrupter of youth.

Plato, however, also makes another, more subtle case against literature, one that focuses less on reading than on performance.

According to this argument, it is not the content of literature that is dangerous, it is the very activity of performance—in Athens, lyric and epic poetry were recited aloud, and could thus be considered "mimetic" arts, like tragedy and comedy. To Socrates, this kind of role-playing was destructive of the integrity of the self: "the same person will hardly be able to play a serious part in life, and at the same time to be an imitator and imitate many other parts as well." To open oneself to the imaginary selves of literature, on this view, is to invite moral contamination. In the end, Plato writes, the poet-performer risks losing his own self entirely, becoming merely a repertory of roles and effects:

> the sort of character who will narrate anything, and, the worse the lie is, the more unscrupulous he will be; nothing will be too bad for him: and he will be ready to imitate anything, not as a joke, but in right good earnest, and before a large company. As I was just now saying, he will attempt to represent the roll of thunder, the noise of wind and hail, or the creaking of wheels, and pulleys, and the various sounds of flutes, pipes, trumpets, and all sorts of instruments: he will bark like a dog, bleat like a sheep, or crow like a cock; his entire art will consist in imitation of voice and gesture.

Trilling does not cite this passage anywhere in his work, but there is no doubt that he must have recognized in it the direct precursor to *Rameau's Nephew*. When Diderot describes the way the nephew "performs" a piece of music, he almost paraphrases

Plato: "With swollen cheeks and a somber throaty sound, he would give us the horns and bassoons. For the oboes he assumed a shrill yet nasal voice," and so on through the whole orchestra. And it is Diderot's dialogue which Trilling locates at the origin of modern literature, fascinated as it is by baseness and impersonation and the splitting of the self. How can Trilling reconcile his nostalgia for Socrates with his instinctive admiration for Rameau, his ethical mistrust of literature with his recognition that literature is the medium of his being?

Trilling's best attempt at an answer comes in his second essay collection, *The Opposing Self,* published in 1955. It is, characteristically, a dialectical answer: rather than side with literature or against it, Trilling looks for those moments in nineteenth-century poetry and fiction when literature seems to take sides against itself. For this reason, the title of the book gives a misleading impression of its contents. The opposing self, what Trilling calls "the modern self . . . characterized by certain powers of indignant perception," by "its intense and adverse imagination of the culture in which it has its being," is not his subject but his premise. Passing up once again the opportunity to write directly about the adversarial masterpieces of modernism, Trilling focuses instead on books and writers who oppose the opposing self—who, with varying degrees of genius and success, try to affirm the social and personal values that modern literature scorns. It is a sign of his creative power as a critic that these occasional pieces—most of which began as introductions to books, from *Little Dorrit* to *Bouvard and Pécuchet*—add up to a coherent, highly personal treatment of his great theme.

The fact that affirmation is an uphill battle for a critic like Trilling becomes clear in the essay "William Dean Howells and the Roots of Modern Taste." Trilling is drawn to Howells for the very reason that American literary history is not drawn to him: because of his principled rejection of the extreme, his love of what he called, admiringly, "the commonplace." "The commonplace," Howells wrote, "is just that light, impalpable, aerial essence which [the novelists] have never got into their confounded books yet." His own novels deal with such mundane, middle-class subjects as apartment-hunting (in *A Hazard of New Fortunes*)—with, in Trilling's words, "the family budget, nagging wives, daughters who want to marry fools, and the difficulties of deciding whom to invite to dinner." The kind of bourgeois existence that Lawrence savagely ridiculed, Howells saw as worthy of the dignity of fiction. Conversely, in Henry James's view, Howells had a "small . . . perception of evil," the kind of evil that so fascinated James himself.

Trilling would very much like to be able to say that, out of these bourgeois materials, Howells made great fiction. According to most modern writers, the self is in love with "the unconditioned" and desires to live the life of "pure spirit," which places it in permanent opposition to society, family, and tradition. It follows that "family men" are "by definition cut off from the true realities of the spirit"—a principle that leaves Trilling, like most readers who are also spouses and parents, facing the irreconcilability of their spiritual aspirations with their everyday lives. It would be a kind of vindication, then, to find in Howells the poet of "the commonplace of the conditioned as we know it in our families": it would be a proof that the bourgeois reader does not have to live in contradiction with himself, that the spirit can blossom in the midst of the quotidian. It would also be a moral relief to find a great novelist who is not enthralled by evil, who does not share the modern belief "that evil is of the very essence of reality."

Yet Trilling is too honest a reader to say that Howells actually is the novelist he longs for. With the best will in the world, he can't escape the feeling that Howells "cannot now engage us, that we cannot expect a revival of interest in him." This may be, he concludes, more of an adverse judgment on the modern reader, who finds Howell's quietness and moderation insipid, than on the writer himself, but it is a judgment that cannot "be legislated or criticized out of existence." When a critic's ideals contradict his experience, it is the experience that must prevail.

Just such an experience of readerly frustration lies at the center of the most important piece in *The Opposing Self,* Trilling's essay on *Mansfield Park.* Jane Austen, of course, is not open to the objection that Trilling allows against Howells, of being simply a not very interesting writer. On the contrary, she is one of Trilling's favorite novelists, and one of his favorite critical subjects—three of his essays, as well as a section of *Sincerity and Authenticity,* are devoted to Austen. Just as significant, he writes, is that she is extremely popular. When he offered a seminar on Austen in the early 1970s, Trilling recalls in "Why We Read Jane Austen," 150 students tried to get in, and fought for the privilege with "almost hysterical moral urgency." Modern readers, even students growing up in post-1960s America, feel that Austen's chronicles of money and marriage in Regency England have something crucial to say to them. For this reason, he writes in "Emma and the Legend of Jane Austen," "the opinions which are held of her work are almost as interesting, and almost as important to think about, as the work itself."

The essay on *Mansfield Park* is occasioned, in fact, by what looks like an anomaly in critical opinion. Readers who love Austen's other novels, Trilling writes, are strangely repelled by this one: "*Mansfield Park* is . . . held by many to be the novel that is least representative of Jane Austen's peculiar attractiveness. For those who admire her it is likely to make an occasion for embarrassment." And the main reason for this embarrassment lies with the novel's main character, Fanny Price: "Nobody, I believe, has ever found it possible to like the heroine of *Mansfield Park.*"

To understand the basis of this objection, which Trilling himself clearly shares, it is useful to compare Fanny with Emma Woodhouse, the heroine of the novel that Austen wrote immediately following *Mansfield Park*. In his essay on *Emma*, Trilling writes of the powerful affection that readers feel for Emma Woodhouse: "inevitably we are attracted to her, we are drawn by her energy and style, and by the intelligence they generate." It's a measure of this attraction that the reader continues to like Emma even as she says and does a whole series of reprehensible things—her errors are, indeed, the whole plot of the novel. Out of snobbery, she forces Harriet Smith to rebuff the honest farmer, Robert Martin, in hopes of landing the shallow, obnoxious vicar, Mr. Elton; out of jealousy, she is cold to Jane Fairfax; out of vanity, she convinces herself that Frank Churchill is in love with her.

Finally, as every reader of *Emma* will remember, she is thoughtlessly cruel to Miss Bates, the poor, good-hearted spinster whose foolish chatter provides one of the book's best sources of comedy. During a picnic, Emma insists that everyone say something to entertain her: "either one thing very clever, be it prose or verse, original or repeated; or two things moderately clever; or three things very dull indeed," as Frank Churchill jokingly demands. When Miss Bates, with typical self-deprecation, says "I shall be sure to say three dull things as soon as ever I open my mouth," Emma replies, "Ah, ma'am, but there may be a difficulty. Pardon me, but you will be limited as to the number—only three at once."

The scene is so memorable because it is perfectly designed to express the moral dilemma at the novel's core. Emma's great vividness and appeal as a character come from just this insistence that people should be interesting, and that her own life should be significant and dramatic. All her matchmaking and interfering comes from her desire to arrange life according to an ideal pattern, and as Trilling writes, this is, "in essence, a poet's demand." Emma is "truly creative," an artist of her own life, and it is Miss Bates's inability to fit into Emma's imagination of a distinguished life that makes her a natural target of scorn.

Emma's mockery of Miss Bates marks the only time in the book when Mr. Knightley, who is clearly Emma's conscience and the novel's, gets genuinely angry with her. When he tells her, "It was badly done, indeed!" the reader flinches along with her. Yet neither Mr. Knightley nor the reader ever truly dislikes Emma. It is impossible for her to lose our sympathy, even when she comes out with some of the awful opinions that Trilling quotes in his essay: for instance, when she says that she can have no interest in a farmer like Robert Martin, because "a farmer can need none of my help, and is therefore in one sense as much above my notice as in every other sense he is below it." This,

Trilling writes, "is carefully contrived by the author to seem as dreadful as possible." Yet the reader always feels that Emma needs only correcting and educating, never punishment.

The reason for this, Trilling argues, is that Emma's "creative" attitude toward her own life is the modern ideal, which the reader inevitably shares. Trilling proposes that we, like Emma, believe that we must make our lives distinguished and exciting, in order to prove our essential worth: we all want to be Emma, the heroine and artist of her life, and dread being Miss Bates, a charmless bit player in someone else's story. If Emma is cruel, it is at least the charismatic cruelty of strength, which can't truly revolt us, because our ultimate grounds of judgment on our own lives are not ethical but aesthetic.

In "Emma and the Legend of Jane Austen," Trilling describes this attitude as the modern "necessity of self-conscious definition and self-criticism, the need to make private judgments of reality." But in "Mansfield Park," he has another name for it: he calls it "the Terror," and names Jane Austen as "an agent of the Terror." This is a deliberate provocation, designed to shock the reader who is used to thinking of Austen as a quaint or endearing writer—what he calls "the people who admire her for the wrong reasons and in the wrong language and thus create a false image of her." Today, this image of Austen is most effectively propagated by the movie adaptations of her books, with their middle-brow, period-piece charm. To Trilling, however, Austen is above all a modern novelist, which means that she has a spiritual affinity with the more overtly terrible writers who came after her—the ones who feature on his syllabus of terrors. If modern literature, as Trilling says, "asks us if we are content with our marriages, with our family lives, with our professional lives, with our friends," then Austen is absolutely modern, even though her questions are asked with more reserve, and admit of happier answers, than Nietzsche's or Freud's. Emma's demand on life is a "poet's demand," and the modern compulsion to conceive life poetically is the source of the Terror.

But what if you were to resist that compulsion, and all the accompanying pressure to be vivid, clever, and distinctive—the pressure to "make private judgments of reality"? What if, instead, you accepted without reservation the old standards of behavior that insisted on submission, modesty, and integrity—especially for women—because they conceived of life as an ethical and religious phenomenon, not an aesthetic one?

Then, Trilling suggests, you would be Fanny Price. Fanny is Emma's exact opposite: she has no energy or charm, she wants nothing from life, and she makes no mistakes. "Emma Woodhouse," we learn in the first sentence of her novel, is "handsome, clever, and rich . . . [and] seemed to unite some of the best blessings of existence." Fanny, on the other hand, is sickly and poor. Worse, she is a poor relation in the home of the wealthy Bertram family, adopted by her rich uncle Sir Thomas but never allowed to forget her lowly status. In scene after scene, Fanny is insulted by one of her relatives—usually the odious Mrs. Norris—and bears it with Christian meekness. Sir Thomas means to compliment Fanny when he says that she is "free from willfulness of temper, self-conceit, and every tendency to that independence of spirit which prevails so much in modern days." But such praise can only reinforce the reader's impression that she is, in Trilling's words, "overly virtuous and consciously virtuous."

Yet in the end, Fanny's meekness is rewarded by Austen. She ends up marrying the cousin she has secretly loved, Edmund Bertram, and rising into gentility. In particular, Fanny triumphs over the woman who, in *Mansfield Park,* is her great opposite: Maria Crawford, whom Edmund spends most of the novel hoping to marry. Maria is intelligent, high-spirited, wickedly witty, and rather manipulative; in other words, she is a spiritual sister to Emma Woodhouse. When Maria tells Edmund, who is planning to become a clergyman, "Be honest and poor, by all means—but I shall not envy you. . . . I have a much greater respect for those that are honest and rich," she has exactly the same impudent honesty as Emma. Yet in *Mansfield Park,* Austen's verdict on Maria is pitiless. By the end of the novel, she is shown to have, in Edmund's words, a "blunted delicacy and a corrupted, vitiated mind," to be shallow and heartless, and worst of all for a woman, to place too slight a value on chastity. It is remarkable how completely negative a verdict Austen passes on Maria Crawford, just two years before she created in Emma Woodhouse her most appealing heroine.

What explains this unlovely moralism, which makes *Mansfield Park,* in Trilling's view, "bitterly resented" by Austen's admirers? For Trilling, the key to the novel can be found in the early scenes where the younger Bertrams, taking advantage of Sir Thomas's absence, decide to put on an amateur theatrical performance. The attitudes of the various characters to this plan reveal them completely, and foreshadow the fates that the novel has in store for them. Maria Bertram, although she is engaged to another man, is eager to act the part of the heroine, because it will give her the opportunity to flirt on stage with Henry Crawford; at the end of the novel, Maria will run away with Henry, to the disgrace of the Bertrams. Maria Crawford loves the idea of acting, while Edmund Bertram, with his native dignity, opposes the whole project; but he eventually agrees to take part in the play, just as he nearly succumbs to Mary's bad influence.

Fanny Price, however, is the most anti-theatrical of all. The very idea of taking a bit part in the play leaves her speechless with dread: "I could not act anything if you were to give me the world. No, indeed, I cannot act." There are several reasons for her disapproval: the scandalous nature of the play, *Lovers' Vows,* which involves love affairs and illegitimate children; the opportunity it will provide for Henry Crawford to seduce Maria Bertram; the expense and disorganization of building a stage, which all the children know their father would never permit if he were home. But Trilling gives relatively little weight to these overt reasons of Fanny's. What really frightens her, he believes, and what Austen herself wants the reader to understand, is that acting a role is itself perilous. When Fanny says "no, indeed, I cannot act," Trilling hears a Platonic avowal. Like Socrates in the *Republic,* she finds the very idea of impersonation to be morally corrupting.

This implication becomes still clearer when Henry Crawford declares his eagerness to put on a play: "I could be fool enough at this moment to undertake any character that ever was written, from Shylock or Richard III, down to the singing hero of a farce in his scarlet coat and cocked hat. I feel as if I could be anything or everything, as if I could rant and storm or sigh or cut capers, in any tragedy or comedy in the English language." Austen could not have read Diderot, and surely did not know Plato; but her language echoes both of theirs, and so does her ethical code. The man who can act anything, all three believe, could also do anything, because he *is* nothing. And the fate of Henry Crawford proves the point with a vengeance.

A modern reader, Trilling acknowledges, finds it hard to take all this concern about amateur theatricals so seriously. Partly this is due to the enormous change in sexual mores since Austen's time. But this can't be the whole explanation, since even in the novel, the other characters think Fanny is being excessively scrupulous. In fact, this "seemingly absurd episode," Trilling writes, goes to the heart of Austen's radical intention. This is to jolt the reader out of the aesthetic attitude to life, and into the ethical attitude; to replace Emma's "poetic" view of her own life with Fanny's moral view. To do this even temporarily, Trilling concludes, is to realize how great the burden of the modern self really is. "We are likely to feel that this placing of the personality, of the quality of being, at the center of the moral life is a chief glory of spirit in her modern manifestation," he writes, and no one is a greater artist of personality than Austen. "Yet we at times become aware of the terrible strain it imposes upon us, of the exhausting effort which the concept of personality requires us to make." To believe, as Fanny Price does, that acting any kind of a part is a sin, that humility and goodness are superior to brilliance and creativity, is itself to sin against the modern spirit in the most audacious way. In our distaste for *Mansfield Park*, Trilling suggests, we can measure our distance from its antique, serene morality—which nevertheless, he insists, "speaks to our secret inexpressible hopes."

According to Schiller, the innocence of nature and antiquity appeals to the modern spirit because "they are what we were; they are what we ought to become once more." The sentimental artist, who sets out self-consciously to recapture that innocence, may never fully achieve it, but there is a nobility in this striving that the naïve artist can never attain. That is why, Schiller writes, the sentimental or modern or adult mind regards the naïve, natural mind with mixed feelings, "in which joyous mockery, respect, and melancholy flow together." Just this ambivalence marks Trilling's feelings about Fanny Price and *Mansfield Park,* and his essay closes *The Opposing Self* on a somber note. If Fanny really "discovers in principle the path to the wholeness of the self which is peace," then the reader's instinctive dislike of Fanny seems to suggest that it would be difficult, if not impossible, to follow her down that path.

But could there be another, more attractive kind of wholeness, one born not of weakness and submission but of strength and mastery? That is the happy possibility Trilling considers in the warmest, most celebratory essay he ever wrote, "The Poet as Hero: Keats in His Letters." To write about Keats's letters rather than his poems was only partly Trilling's choice: the essay was written as the introduction to a new edition of the letters. But it is nonetheless characteristic of Trilling to be less interested in Keats's poetry than in his moral example, which rests on his life and thought as well as his work. "We think of him as something even more interesting than a poet, we think of him as a man," Trilling writes, and "his being a poet was his chosen way of being a man."

This way of thinking about artistic vocation, not as a withdrawal from the common life but as a tool for confronting that life, is fundamental to the way Trilling reads literature. His own experience as a creative writer meant that, while he fully understood the rarity and difficulty of artistic creation, he did not hold it in superstitious awe. He knew that "the mind that creates" is not mysteriously separate from "the man who suffers," as T. S. Eliot had written in "Tradition and the Individual Talent." In fact, if modernism is grounded on this sort of division—between personality and impersonality, life and art, history and the ideal—Keats stands for the possibility of wholeness and reconciliation.

"The great and remarkable thing about Keats," Trilling writes, "is that he did not refine by negation but by natural growth." Indeed, he argues, one of the things that has consistently made readers underestimate Keats is the modern belief that negation and criticism are the prerequisites of artistic seriousness. For instance, "we are ambivalent in our conception of the moral status of eating and drinking," Trilling writes, and we tend to think of oral pleasure as infantile and passive. But Keats writes with undisguised pleasure about eating, and in one letter famously describes the pleasure of eating a nectarine: "it went down soft, slushy, oozy . . . like a beatified strawberry." Similarly, modern writers are usually suspicious of the family, as a breeding ground of neurosis and a restraint on personal autonomy. But Keats's "family feeling was enormously strong and perfectly direct," and some of his greatest letters were written to his siblings.

Trilling sums up these facets of Keats's character with the word "geniality," which he chooses precisely because it has a rather insipid sound to contemporary ears. To be genial, today, means to be inoffensively friendly. But Trilling points to the origin of geniality in the word "genius," and suggests that the Romantic era was a time when genius and geniality, in the sense of "simple good-humoredness and sociability," could still go together. At the same time, he does not scant the darkness of Keats's life and personality—his pride and jealousy, his sickness and early death. Indeed, few writers have known as much suffering and injustice as Keats. What impresses Trilling is that the poet was able to meet the experience of evil with a strong impulse of affirmation. Health and friendship and pleasure were as real to him as their opposites. This is what separates writers like Keats—and, Trilling adds, Shakespeare—from a modernist master like Kafka, for whom "knowledge of evil exists without the contradictory knowledge of the self in its health and validity."

It is significant that, for Trilling, the opposite of the knowledge of evil is not the knowledge of good, but knowledge of the self. This is a concession to what Trilling thinks of as a necessary modern skepticism. It is no longer credible, he implies, to see the world as one in which good and evil are essentially in balance, thanks to a benevolent Providence. If there is to be an affirmative force to resist our overwhelming awareness of evil, it must come from within, from a personality so strong and vital that it can cope with suffering and, in a sense, redeem it. This redemption, in Keats's famous phrase, takes the form of "soul-making," and Trilling quotes the letter of 1819 in which Keats describes the world as, not a vale of tears, but a vale of soul-making: "Do you not see how necessary a World of Pains and troubles is to school an Intelligence and make it a soul?"

The self—which Keats calls, for honorific rather than religious purposes, the soul—is something made, not given; it is a work, like a work of art. But just as, to Trilling, Keats the man is greater than Keats the poet, so to Keats, making a self is a greater achievement than making a poem. Poetry is "not so fine a thing as philosophy," Keats wrote in another letter, "for the same reason that an eagle is not so fine a thing as a truth." It makes sense that Trilling quotes this phrase on several occasions in his writing, since so much of his criticism grapples with the insistence of modern literature that an eagle beats a truth every time. Di Grasso's leap, Blake's road of excess, Nietzsche's Dionysus: each of these is a way of exalting genius above goodness.

"The peculiar bitterness of modern man," Trilling writes in *Sincerity and Authenticity,* is "the knowledge that he is not a genius"—a bitterness that Trilling knew intimately, and so was perfectly equipped to diagnose. If artistic genius is required

to live a fully human existence, then almost everyone is condemned to despair, like Rameau's nephew. But if Keats is right,
if the soul is a greater creation than any poem, then every
human being can have a share in the dignity of creation. Not
everyone has a self, in this elevated sense of the word, but
anyone can choose to make a self. To Trilling, literature was
above all the medium in which he made himself, and his essays,
with all their dignity and vulnerability, are the record of a soul
being made through its confrontation with texts. For this reason, Trilling may matter most of all as a representative of the
virtue he admired in George Orwell: "the virtue of not being
a genius."

8
the
reader
as hero

Walt Whitman is not a writer ordinarily associated with Lionel Trilling. It may even seem paradoxical to mention them together: the critic's formality and irony seem to stand at the opposite pole from the poet's ardor and adhesiveness. But in 1945, at the end of the Second World War, Trilling wrote a short article about Whitman in *The Nation,* in which he quoted a phrase from *Democratic Vistas* that captures the central intuition of his criticism: "There is, in sanest hours, a consciousness, a thought that rises, independent, lifted out from all else, calm, like the stars, shining, eternal. This is the thought of identity—yours for you, whoever you are, as mine for me. Miracle of miracles, beyond statement, most spiritual of earth's dreams, yet hardest basic fact, and only entrance to all facts."

Whitman's "identity" is not quite the same as Keats's "soul" —the first seems like a gift, while the second is an object of labor—but it is significant that Trilling is drawn to them both. For the self, to use his own preferred term, emerges in his late work as the real object of Trilling's study. Whitman "knows how [identity] can be generated. Literature can generate it," Trilling writes, and the permanent value of his own criticism is as a record of the way literature generates a self. Reading Arnold and Forster, Trilling weighed the strengths of liberalism against its weaknesses, the power of art against its irresponsibility, and struck a balance by committing himself to moral realism and the liberal imagination. Reading Diderot and Nietzsche and Freud, he acknowledged the right of modern literature to demolish all conventions—what Yeats called, in "Meru," "Ravening, raging, and uprooting that he may come / Into the desolation of reality." Yet reading Keats and Austen, he imagined ways to reaffirm, sternly or joyfully, the values that modern literature denies. And in his career as a novelist and teacher, he found himself living out the same dilemmas he encountered in his reading: the contesting rights of rebellion and responsibility, the will and the conscience. What he wrote about Henry James is also true of himself: "Try as we may, we cannot down our experience of . . . the man, the man-writing—he becomes part of our experience of his work, which we see not as a collocation of particular aesthetic objects but as an intention, the enterprise of a lifetime, which has its own coherence and form and is thus itself an aesthetic object of a kind."

Toward the end of his life, however, the cultural ground began to shift under Trilling's feet, in ways that put this very conception of literature and selfhood in jeopardy. In *Beyond Culture* (1965) and *Sincerity and Authenticity* (1971), and the late essays collected after his death in *The Last Decade,* Trilling registers these cultural changes in indirect and uneasy ways. It would be easy to say that what he is responding to is "the Sixties," and this would not be wrong, just as it's not wrong to say that *The Liberal Imagination* is about the Popular Front and the Cold War. But as always, Trilling deliberately avoids casting his work as a response to immediate issues. This does not mean that he was unaware of them. In 1968, for instance, when students occupied buildings at Columbia University—including Hamilton Hall, where the English department was located— Trilling was appointed to the faculty committee in charge of investigating the disturbances and responding to student demands. He was, by then, a kind of living symbol of the university, and as such a major target for protestors: Diana Trilling recalled that one "zealot . . . distributed on the Columbia campus a poster of the kind which is displayed in post offices with pictures of dangerous criminals: below a photograph of Lionel was the legend, WANTED, DEAD OR ALIVE. FOR CRIMES AGAINST HUMANITY."

But while Trilling was surely thinking of such experiences when he refers to "the case against mind that is now being openly litigated in our culture," in his 1972 lecture "Mind in the Modern World," he made a great effort not to become embroiled in the campus culture wars. Even so, in the 1970s and 1980s, combatants in those wars—from Philip Rieff to Gertrude Himmelfarb—would enlist Trilling as a spiritual ally. Some, like Norman Podhoretz, would even blame him for not being forthright enough about his views of the counterculture, affirmative action, the literary canon, and other topics of controversy.

Now that those battles are themselves passing into history, however, it is easier to see that Trilling's way of dealing with them, in his work of the 1960s and 1970s, was deliberate and justified. With a few exceptions—as when he worries about the effects of affirmative action in "Mind in the Modern World"— Trilling avoids talking directly about political issues. Instead, he tries to make sense of cultural changes in personal, literary terms—to make them an object of experience, rather than a subject for debate. And for this very reason, he was able to see further into the future than most of his contemporaries. He understood that what was changing in the 1960s was of deeper import than the counterculture or multiculturalism. Instead, he speaks directly to our current loss of faith in literature— *2* which is, as he understood, fundamentally a loss of faith in a certain ideal of selfhood.

To see how Trilling addressed the events of the 1960s through the medium of literature, the best place to start is his essay "Aggression and Utopia," written in 1971 as a paper for a psychoanalytic conference. His subject is William Morris's 1890 novel *News from Nowhere,* a "utopian romance" about a socialist future in which human life has been perfected. The narrator, who has gone to bed after spending the evening at a fruitless debate among a handful of committed revolutionaries, dreams that he has woken up in the twenty-first century, to find that class exploitation has been abolished, along with money, pollution, law, and politics ("I will answer your question briefly by saying that we are very well off as to politics—because we have none," one character explains). Even death has been at least postponed, since the human lifespan is greatly increased.

The novel's subtitle is "an epoch of rest," and Morris holds up perfect restfulness as his ideal. In his utopia, Trilling summarizes, "life is lived without urgency and without anxiety. It is lived for itself alone, for its own delight in itself." Another way of putting it is that, in such a life, there is no room for aggression. In this, Morris seems to speak directly to, and for, the aspirations of the students of the 1960s. "Over the last decade,"

Trilling writes, "many people, young people especially, have come to share Morris's certitude about the feasibility of extirpating aggression." It follows that, when Trilling voices his doubts about Morris's novel, he is also addressing the ideals of the flower children and the anti-war movement.

The clue that there may be a price to pay for the abolition of aggression comes when Morris discusses the arts in his utopia. An old man confronts the narrator with a question about the literature of the bad old days, before the Revolution:

> "You see, I have read not a few books of the past days, and certainly they are much more alive than those which are written now; and good sound unlimited competition was the condition under which they were written—if we didn't know that from the record book of history, we should know it from the books themselves. There is a spirit of adventure in them and signs of a capacity to extract good out of evil which our literature quite lacks now; and I cannot help thinking that our moralists and historians exaggerate hugely the unhappiness of the past days, in which such splendid works of imagination and intellect were produced."

Great art, Morris concedes, is a product of the competitive will, or at least a byproduct of it. This agrees wholly with Trilling's own view, of course: no one was more alert to the egotism and will-to-power of great writers. For Morris, however, the sacrifice of this kind of art is a price well worth paying for utopia, and the narrator replies to the old man's speech with a rebuke: "You wouldn't talk so if you had any idea of our life. To me you seem here as if you were living in heaven compared with us of the country from which I came." And Trilling believes that this disparaging attitude toward art and struggle is becoming "an active ideal" in the America of the 1960s and '70s. A masterpiece, after all, requires mastery, and mastery is not compatible with peacefulness or equality: "there is . . . a tendency to identify with the aggression imputed to nationalism and capitalism that element of 'fighting' which, in the cultural tradition of the West, has been thought essential to the artistic life."

And not just to the artistic life. According to Keats, one must endure "a world of pains and troubles," not just to create a work of art, but to create a soul. To Trilling, literature matters because it involves the reader in this kind of trouble, which is why he imagines reading as a kind of contest: "Our typical experience of a work which will eventually have authority with us is to begin our relation to it at a conscious disadvantage, and to wrestle with it until it consents to bless us," he writes in "The Fate of Pleasure." In that 1963 essay, he observes how uncomfortable modern readers are with the notion, once taken for granted, that a work of art should give pleasure: "We are repelled by the idea of an art that is consumer-directed and comfortable, let alone luxurious."

Yet in the last decade of his life, he noticed that this modern puritanism was starting to turn itself inside out. Perhaps the best way to understand this phase of Trilling's work is to read him alongside the most brilliant critic of the younger generation, Susan Sontag. *Against Interpretation*, Sontag's 1966 essay collection, nowhere mentions Trilling by name, but he represents all the tendencies in literature and criticism that Sontag was rebelling against. When she repeatedly mocks "the Matthew Arnold notion of culture," and the idea of literature as a matter of "reportage and moral judgment," there is no question that Trilling—the biographer of Arnold, the defender of moral realism—is being attacked.

What Sontag offers instead is her celebrated "erotics of art." This is not quite as simple as an art that is "consumer-directed and comfortable," but it is at least an art that desires to give pleasure, that stimulates the senses more than the conscience. "We must learn to see more, to hear more, to feel more," she writes; and again, "Art is not only about something; it is something." The epitome of this kind of art, in *Against Interpretation* at least, is Jack Smith's experimental film *Flaming Creatures*, with its "childlike and witty" sexual tableaux. "Smith's film is strictly a treat for the senses," Sontag writes. "In this it is the very opposite of a 'literary' film." In fact, with its refusal of repression and celebration of sexual innocence—what Sontag calls its "gaiety" and "ingenuousness"—it is a product of much the same Sixties sensibility that Trilling saw as allied to William Morris.

At other moments in *Against Interpretation*, however, Sontag shows that she can also be sympathetic to the older modernist argument against pleasure. In "One Culture and the New Sensibility," she once again argues that "the most interesting works of contemporary art . . . are adventures in sensation," but now this sensation no longer seems like a "treat for the senses"; instead, it is "a kind of shock therapy for both confounding and unclosing our senses." And the reader or viewer or listener should no more expect to enjoy this process than the patient enjoys shock therapy. "The new art is anti-hedonistic," Sontag writes, it "hurts," it is "boring" and "frustrating." To appreciate contemporary artists like Mark Rothko and Morton Feldman and Merce Cunningham, she explains, "demand[s] an education of sensibility whose difficulties and length of apprenticeship are at least comparable to the difficulties of mastering physics or engineering."

To Trilling, this sort of demand, while extreme, is quite familiar. He sees it as the latest version of the modern deprecation of beauty, a tendency that can be seen as early as Edmund Burke's elevation of the sublime over the beautiful. In *Sincerity and Authenticity,* he writes that Sontag's contention "that pleasure has nothing to do with the artistic experience . . . takes us a little but not wholly aback," since it "has had its ground prepared by two centuries of aesthetic theory and artistic practice." Yet the strange thing about Sontag's "One Culture" is that it seems just as hospitable to the simplest pleasures as to the most complicated unpleasure. The same intellectual who has to take a Ph.D. in contemporary art, she writes, is also ready to enjoy "the singing style of Dionne Warwick" or "the personalities and music of the Beatles," and not just as a vacation from strenuousness: "they are experienced without condescension." "The new sensibility is defiantly pluralistic," she concludes, "it is dedicated both to an excruciating seriousness and to fun and wit and nostalgia."

Sontag was prescient. Her "one culture" has become our culture, her "new sensibility" the predominant sensibility of our time. When Louis Menand—to return to his introduction to *The Liberal Imagination*—writes that "since the 1960s . . . educated people tend to be culturally promiscuous and permissive. They don't use the language of approval and disapproval in their responses; they simply like some experiences and dislike other experiences," he is testifying to the triumph of the new sensibility. But he also reveals an aspect of that sensibility which Sontag herself did not fully anticipate. This is the fact that the basis of our catholicity is not universal enthusiasm, but a tolerant diffidence toward all kinds of art. Trilling, Menand writes, "worried too much about culture"; today, we don't have to worry, because culture does not greatly affect us, for good or bad. As with any other commodity in our consumer society, we can take it or leave it according to taste.

Here, Trilling was more far-seeing than Sontag herself. What she welcomed as a new expansion of possibilities—and with some justice: who doesn't like the Beatles?—he recognized as an essential disengagement from the experience of art. In a footnote to *Sincerity and Authenticity,* he anticipated Menand by some thirty-five years: "At the present moment, art cannot be said to make exigent demands upon the audience. That segment of our culture which is at all permeable to contemporary art is wholly permeable by it. . . . The audience likes or does not like, is pleased or not pleased—the faculty of 'taste' has reestablished itself at the center of the experience of art."

Paradoxically, Trilling recognized, it is this very permeability that explains the readiness of the "new sensibility" to expose itself to difficult and tedious works. If the self does not have to offer any resistance to what it reads, hears, and sees—even the kind of resistance that precedes acceptance, the "wrestling" that Trilling saw as the prelude to receiving a work's "blessing"— then it is actually just as easy to experience Morton Feldman as the Beatles. That is because the nature of the experience has changed: art is no longer the medium through which the self defines itself, but an object of consumption. The metaphor of taste already implies that the purpose of the work of art is to be consumed, which also means, consumed away, used up and gotten rid of.

Trilling was especially acute in recognizing that this sort of cultural consumption was already becoming the basis of a new kind of self-definition. In the twenty-first century, it has become a truism that people define themselves by their purchases, their "brand loyalties." But this kind of definition-by-consumption now extends far beyond the old types of tangible commodities—the kind of car you drive, say, or the kind of clothes you wear. It is above all in the realm of culture, or "content," that brand loyalties matter. There are intricate gradations of prestige involved in listening to the right music, liking the right movies, even living in the coolest neighborhood. The phenomena of the "fanboy" and the "hipster," both social types defined entirely by their allegiance to certain kinds of nontangible goods, is indicative of the way cultural consumption is used as a basis—or, perhaps, a substitute?—for identity. It may not be too much to say that the division of American politics into "red" and "blue" states is really a division into states of mind, and that the cultural preferences of these opponents are ultimately more salient than their political allegiances.

All of this Trilling was able to predict in the late 1960s and early 1970s—once again, by reading politics and culture through the lens of literature. In his 1973 lecture "Art, Will, and Necessity," he observed that "the highest achievement of the free subversive spirit has been coopted to lend the color of spirituality to the capitalist enterprise." In "The Fate of Pleasure," he describes how "our high culture invites us to transfer our energies from the bourgeois competition to the spiritual competition"—a competition that is "not without its own peculiar sordidness and absurdity." And in his essay "The Two Environments"—written in 1965, the same year as Sontag's "One Culture and the New Sensibility"—he summed up the whole career of the culture industry from that time to this: "The economy itself is deeply involved with matters of style and with the conditions of the spirit or psyche. Our commodities are not only mere *things* but states of mind: joy, freedom, self-definition, self-esteem. . . . Advertising joins with literature in agitating the question of who one is, of what kind of person one should want to be, a choice in which one's possessions and appearance, one's tastes, are as important as one's feelings and behavior."

It is no accident, finally, that the age of the new sensibility, of total permeability to art, of the commodification of spiritual prestige, is also the age of literature's crisis of confidence. As Sontag already saw in 1965, "the primary feature of the new sensibility is that its model product is not the literary work, above all, the novel." To Sontag, the superiority of the performing and visual arts has to do with their freedom from literature's "heavy burden of 'content,' both reportage and moral judgment." Music, film, and dance are better able to provide new "sensory mixes" than the novel, with its "ideas" and "moral sentiments."

Trilling agreed with this diagnosis, though he took a much

less sanguine view of it than Sontag. Throughout his life, Trilling had been accustomed to treating literature as the medium of experience. To the extent that his criticism takes sides in various arguments—having to do with liberalism and radicalism, the artist and the bourgeois, negation and affirmation—these are arguments conducted in and through literature, and having as their ultimate reference the nature of the self, and of his own self.

As with Whitman, one does not usually think of John Dewey as a writer who was important to Trilling, but just as he liked to quote Whitman on identity, so he liked to quote Dewey on character: "What makes the supreme appeal to him? What sort of an agent, of a person, shall he be? This is the question finally at stake in any genuinely moral situation: What shall the agent *be*? What sort of a character shall he assume? . . . When ends are genuinely incompatible, no common denominator can be found except by deciding what sort of character is most highly prized and shall be given supremacy."

Trilling refers to this passage on at least three occasions—a sign of how well it captures the process of his own thought. Moral thinking, for Trilling, is finally thinking about the kind of character one wants to have. And having a character, as Dewey suggests, is bound up with being a character. This does not mean that life is a work of art, or that one should live as if one were the hero of a novel—a delusion that has itself been a favorite theme of novels, from *Don Quixote* to *Madame Bovary*. If the self is a kind of character, this is rather because it is consistent with itself, because it remains unitary even as it develops toward a goal, and because it aspires to be good and beautiful, as the best characters are. The self is the protagonist of its own life, because life itself is a kind of *agon*, a struggle, which can be judged as well or badly conducted, as noble or base.

This is what Trilling refers to, in "Art, Will, and Necessity," as "the realization of self through self-knowledge, the forming of an autonomous personal character." And it is this concept of the self that, to his dismay, Trilling sees losing purchase in American culture. Writing about *News from Nowhere,* he notes that Morris's utopia dispenses with "an assumption which is integral to high Western culture: that man's nature and destiny are fulfilled not through his success in achieving pleasure but through setting himself goals which are beyond pleasure." Traditionally, the struggle toward these goals is what provided man's "sense of his largeness of spirit, his dignity, his transcendent significance."

When Sontag talks about replacing "the eschatology of transcendence" with "the eschatology of immanence," she once again bears out Trilling's sense that the demotion of literature is part of a larger demotion of the self. It is not coincidental that this phrase comes in an essay about Norman O. Brown, in which she sympathizes with Brown's sexual-liberationist critique of Freud: "Revolutionary mind that he was, Freud nevertheless supported the perennial aspirations of repressive culture." Trilling, too, recognizes the figure of Freud at the very center of this debate over the future of literature and the self. Despite all his disagreements with Freud, what Trilling finally prizes in him is precisely his linking of aspiration with repression. "Freud, in insisting upon the essential immitigability of the human condition . . . had the intention of sustaining the authenticity of human existence that formerly had been ratified by God," Trilling writes in *Sincerity and Authenticity*.

Trilling is a humanist in the tradition of Freud, sharing his "faith quite unrelated to hope" and "piety that takes virtually the form of pride": a faith that human existence is a fate, a pride in the way fate shapes and is shaped by character. Put this way, it is possible to see the connection between Freud and Trilling's other master, Arnold, and to understand why this humanist faith is so deeply implicated in literature. When the self has been replaced by the new sensibility, literature can no longer matter as it used to do.

"The extreme attenuation of the authority of literary culture," Trilling observed in the early 1970s, is related to the declining interest in narrative and in the hero, since "the hero is his history from his significant birth to his significant death." The hero of story exists only in story, but the sense that each of us is the protagonist of his or her own life is nurtured by those stories, and nurtures them. And the "attenuation" of the self will inevitably have consequences that go beyond the literary. In the view of one critic, in fact, the 1960s marked "a sea-change in the whole culture, a transvaluation of values—for which there are many names. Barbarism is one name for what was taking over. Let's use Nietzsche's term: we had entered, really entered, the age of nihilism."

So wrote Susan Sontag, in 1996, in an afterword to the thirtieth anniversary edition of *Against Interpretation*. "The ever more triumphant values of consumer capitalism promote—indeed, impose—the cultural mixes and insolence and defense of pleasure that I was advocating for quite different reasons," she saw in retrospect. Trilling, of course, saw this even at the time. But what makes his work so valuable, and so heartening, is that he did not allow this cultural change to turn him into a culture warrior. He knew that literature's victories are always achieved against the larger circumstance of defeat, that to live a literary life—which also means, to live life according to the disciplines of literature—is itself the best, most inspiriting resistance to an unliterary culture. And his writing, by showing what it means to define one's self through reading, proves that this kind of readerly heroism is always a possibility for those who believe in it. The most important reason why Trilling matters for our time is that he helps us, to quote his own praise of the sociologist David Riesman, to assert what in our day will seem a difficult idea even to people of great moral sensitivity—that one may live a real life apart from the group, that one may exist as an actual person not only at the center of society but on its margins, that one's values may be none the less real and valuable because they do not prevail and are even rejected and submerged. . . . That this needs to be said suggests the peculiar threat to the individual that our society offers.

acknowledgments

I am happy to have this chance to thank Alana Newhouse and Gabriel Sanders, my editors at *Tablet* magazine, for all their encouragement and support. To Leon Wieseltier, I am happily indebted not just for the chance to return to *The New Republic* as a senior editor, but for his friendship and guidance over the last fifteen years. Leon has helped to transmit Trilling's legacy to me and many others, not just as editor of Trilling's essays, but as a constant champion of the intellectual virtues of "variousness, possibility, complexity, and difficulty." I certainly would never have written this book without the introduction to Trilling, and many other things, he gave me.

Teaching a seminar on the New York Intellectuals at Columbia University—in Trilling's old building, Hamilton Hall—was crucial for developing my thoughts about Trilling and how he fit into, and stood apart from, his milieu. I am grateful to Jeremy Dauber, director of Columbia University's Institute for Israel and Jewish Studies, and to Andrew Delbanco, director of Columbia's American Studies program, for giving me this opportunity.

Thanks to Ted Genoways, editor of *Virginia Quarterly Review,* and Abraham Socher, editor of the *Jewish Review of Books,* for publishing sections of *Why Trilling Matters* in an earlier form. And thanks to those who shared their ideas and stories about Trilling with me, including Ruth Wisse, Gerald Howard, and Morris Dickstein.

I am grateful to Ileene Smith, editor of Yale University Press's "Why X Matters" series, for agreeing to my proposal for a book on Trilling, and for bringing it to fruition.

I first met Jonathan Rosen in 1999, when he invited me to become poetry editor of the *Forward*; as it turned out, this was just the first of many times I would experience his generosity and encouragement, most recently as editor of my book on Benjamin Disraeli for Nextbook's Jewish Encounters series. In print and in person, Jonathan's thinking about the connection between Jewishness and Americanness, politics and literature, has been an important influence on me. And as a friend, I have admired and learned from his rare combination of intellect and *menschlichkeit.* I'm proud to be able to dedicate *Why Trilling Matters* to him.

index

artistic will: concepts of justice vs., 22, 57–58, 67, 69, 124, 125; critical responses to, 51–53; Morris's utopia vs., 156–57; serious reader's response to, 5, 109; service to greater good of, 62–63, 147, 152; truth and, 68–69; wholesome acceptance and, 146–50

Asch, Nathan, *Pay Day,* 46

Atwood, Margaret, 4

Auden, W. H., 95

Austen, Jane, 136–46, 152; contemporary relevance and popularity of, 137, 140–41; *Emma,* 138–43; *Mansfield Park,* 136–38, 140–45, 146

Babel, Isaac, 78 84, 86–87, 90, 91–94; "Argamak," 81–82; "The Cemetery in Kozin," 83; "Di Grasso," 91–94, 120, 149; "My First Goose," 81, 91; "Odessa Stories," 80; "The Rebbe," 83; "The Rebbe's Son," 83; *Red Cavalry,* 78–83, 84; "Zamosc," 81

Balzac, Honoré de, 63, 96

barbarism, 167

Barth, John, 2, 18

Baudelaire, Charles, 117

Beatles, 160, 161

Beats, 115, 120; Columbia poetry reading, 114, 115–16

beauty: good and, 130–31; justice and, 67; modern deprecation of, 159

Being, sentiment of, 89

Bellow, Saul, 34, 75

Berlin, Isaiah, 70

bestsellers, 15

Beyond Culture (Trilling), 9, 98, 153; preface, 12

Bialik, Chaim Nachman, "In the City of Slaughter," 82

Blake, William, 112, 121, 149; "Ah, Sunflower," 117–18; Ginsberg vision of, 117–18, 119; "Jerusalem," 28; "Proverbs of Hell," 111–12

books and bookstores, decline of, 3–4, 19

brand loyalties, 162

Brooks, Gwendolyn, 2

Brown, Norman O., 165–66

Burke, Edmund, 159

Butler, Nicholas Murray, 114

Camus, Albert, *The Stranger,* 104

capitalism, 157, 162, 167

Cervantes, Miguel de, *Don Quixote,* 165

Chambers, Whittaker, 26, 38

character, 164–65

Chaucer, Geoffrey, 76

civilization, art and, 31–35, 99–100, 103, 104–6, 107–9, 129

Fitzgerald, F. Scott: *The Great Gatsby*, 96; Trilling essay on, 62–63, 68

Flaming Creatures (film), 158

Flaubert, Gustave, *Madame Bovary*, 165

Ford, Richard, 2

Forster, E. M., 11, 49, 52–56, 58–60, 61, 69, 152; *Howards End*, 59–60; *A Passage to India*, 49; Trilling biography of, 49, 54–55, 56, 58–60

Franzen, Jonathan, 14–15, 16; *The Corrections*, 14–15; "Perchance to Dream," 2, 3, 4, 5, 20

Freud, Sigmund, 6, 102, 107–9, 141, 152, 166; *Civilization and Its Discontents*, 107–8, 122–23; literary interpretation and, 50–51

"Freud and Literature" (Trilling), 50–51

"Function of the Little Magazine, The" (Trilling), 5, 14, 94

Gaddis, William, 15

genius: geniality and, 148; justice as antagonist of, 124, 125; madness linked with, 117, 127; Trilling on self-knowledge about, 149–50

German Romanticism, 130

Gide, André, 45, 94, 95, 98

Ginsberg, Allen, 112–21; "Howl," 115, 118–21, 124–25, 127; sanity and, 115, 117, 127; "Sunflower Sutra," 119; Trilling's relationship with, 112–16, 119, 120–21, 124–27

Ginsberg, Louis, 113, 115

Gioia, Dana, "Does Poetry Matter?," 2, 3, 20

Goethe, Johann Wolfgang von, 102, 109

"good and beautiful," 130–31

Great Depression. *See* Depression

greater good, 62

Greek tragedy, 106

Greenberg, Clement, 78

Hamilton Hall, student takeover (1968) of, 153

happiness, 89, 108, 131

Hawkes, John, 18

Heart of Darkness (Conrad), 104–5, 107, 132

Hegel, G. W. F., 126; *Phenomenology of Spirit*, 102

Hemingway, Ernest, 24, 33

heroism, 63, 166–67; anti-hero and, 103–5

Himmelfarb, Gertrude, 154

Hitler, Adolf, 48

Homer, 132; *Iliad*, 56

Howe, Irving, 8, 14, 73, 78

Howells, William Dean, 135–37; *A Hazard of New Fortunes*, 135–36

literary criticism (*continued*)
51; as cultural authority, 20–21; cultural context and, 50–61; decline of, 3, 14, 19; different approaches to, 9, 50–51; as expression of ideas, 28–29; as expression of sensibility, 9; Forster and, 55; ideals vs. experience and, 136; postmodernist approach to, 17, 18; psychology vs. rhetoric as focus of, 50–51; secular Jews and, 75–76; shared audience for, 97; Sontag and, 158–60; Trilling's contribution to, 10, 25, 32, 69–80, 84, 96–98, 101, 151–52, 164; Trilling's earliest works of, 28–29, 74–75; Wilson's vs. Trilling's approach to, 21–24, 95, 96

"Literary Entrails" (Ozick), 3, 4, 5, 15–16

literary life, 15–17, 19–21, 38; as community, 20–21; decline of, 1–8, 155, 166–67; living of, 17; media substitutes for, 15, 163; political action and, 45; Trilling as emblem of, 4, 8, 10, 157, 167

literature: as academic field, 3, 71–72, 112, 153; audience for, 14–17; criticism's importance to, 20–21; ethical mistrust of, 134; as experience, 10, 21, 164; humanist faith and, 166; liberals and, 38–43, 56–58, 63, 69–70, 94; Platonic critique of, 131–33; selfhood from, 22, 152, 165–66, 167–68; Sontag's demotion of, 163, 165–66; will of artist and, 51–52. *See also* modernism; novel; poetry; reading

little magazines, 4, 5, 14. *See also Commentary; Partisan Review*

Locke, John, 40

love, 63, 68, 70

madness, genius linked with, 117, 127

Mailer, Norman, 34, 75

Malamud, Bernard, 34

"Manifesto" (1932), 45

Mann, Thomas, 31, 75, 94, 95, 97, 98; *Death in Venice,* 104–5, 106, 107, 108, 132

"Manners, Morals, and the Novel" (Trilling), 17, 18–19

Mansfield Park (Austen), 136–38, 140–45, 146; readers' dislike of, 137, 143, 144–45

Marx, Karl, 102

Marxism, 43, 47, 77

Matthew Arnold (Trilling), 37–38, 49–50, 53, 56–57, 58

maturity, 124, 125, 127

media, 15, 163

Menard, Louis, 7, 8, 25, 160

Menorah Journal, 74, 75, 77–78

middle class, 47, 48; Lawrence's ridicule of, 99–100, 135; novels of, 18, 135–36

Middle of the Journey, The (Trilling), 24, 25–29, 121; characters and plot of, 26–28, 59, 65, 71–72; new edition of, 6

Mill, John Stuart, 40; essay praising Coleridge by, 41, 43, 48

Milton, John, 17, 25; *Areopagitica,* 5

mimetic arts, 133

mind, 65–67, 123, 124, 125; as Trilling key word, 11

modernism: American cultural eminence of, 31–34, 44–45, 44–47; anti-hero and, 103–5; approach to aging of, 121–22; Babel and, 83–84, 90, 116; concept of evil and, 104–6, 136; critique of civilization and, 31–35, 99–100, 103–9, 129; European literary conservatives and, 45; golden age (1920s) masters of, 31, 94–98; James and, 63; Jewish identity and, 90; Keats's wholesomeness vs., 147–48; literary explication and, 96, 97; militancy of, 54, 112, 129; moral critique of, 131, 132, 134, 145; personal testimony and, 89, 99–101, 109, 116, 120, 141, 145; rebellion against convention and, 116–17, 152; resistance to, 130–

31; Trilling on teaching literature of, 51, 98–101, 129–30; as Trilling's formative influence, 31–34, 44–45; Trilling's reactions to, 78, 83–84, 89–90, 94–101, 104–6, 109, 116, 121, 129–32, 134, 147, 148–50; view of Wordsworth and, 84–85, 87; Wilson study of, 95, 96

moral, as Trilling key word, 11, 60, 131

morality: character and, 164; Keats as example of, 146–47; primal truth vs., 111–12; style in opposition to, 60–61, 70

moral judgment, 104, 107

Moral Obligation to Be Intelligent (Trilling and Wieseltier, ed), 6

moral realism: James's demonstration of, 66–67; meaning of, 60–61, 64; Trilling's commitment to, 152, 158

moral thinking, 164–65

Morris, William, *News from Nowhere,* 155–58, 165

multiculturalism, 155

Murphy, Geraldine, 25, 29

music, 163

Mussolini, Benito, 48

"My First Goose" (Babel), 81, 91

"myth of sick artist," 117

Nation (magazine), 151

nationalism, 157

naturalism, 47, 64

Nature, sensibility and, 87–88

neoconservatism, 8, 42, 62

New Critics, 51, 95

New Deal liberals, 38

News from Nowhere (Morris), 155–58, 165

newspaper book reviews, 3

New Yorker (magazine), 7

New York intellectuals, 8, 12, 42, 63; Jewish identity and, 71, 73, 76, 77–78

New York Review Books, 6

New York State Psychiatric Institute, 115

New York Times, Trilling front-page obituary, 4

Nietzsche, Friedrich, 108, 126, 141, 149, 152, 167; *The Birth of Tragedy,* 93, 106–7

nihilism, 167

nobility of style, 56–57

novel: American Jewish writers of, 34, 75, 79; anti-hero and, 103–5; character and, 164–65; cultural decline of, 2, 3; egolessness of, 63, 68, 70; ethical vs. aesthetic ideal and, 32–35; familiar conventions of, 13; Forster and, 49, 53–54, 58, 59–60; individual vs. collective values and, 43, 52; Jewish character portrayal in, 76–77; middle-class subjects

and, 18, 135–36; modern masterpieces of, 31; money/status concerns of, 17–18, 62–63; moral realism and, 60–61; readers' connectedness with, 15–17; realism and, 17, 18–19, 42–47, 52, 57, 65; Sontag's view of, 163; Trilling's disappointment as writer of, 6–7, 23–24, 25, 29–33, 49, 51, 69, 90; Trilling's essay on, 17, 18–19

Oates, Joyce Carol, 2

Odessa, 82, 91

"On the Teaching of Modern Literature" (Trilling), 51, 98–101, 121, 129–30

Opposing Self, The (Trilling), 9, 134–50

Orwell, George, 150

Ozick, Cynthia, 20–21, 29–30; "Literary Entrails," 3, 4, 5, 15–16; as Trilling literary successor, 14

Parrington, V. L., 18; *Main Currents in American Thought,* 63

Partisan Review, 4, 12, 14, 71, 96; defense of modernism and, 95; Jewish writers and, 77–78; liberal anti-Communism and, 39, 42; Trilling's journal excerpted in, 24, 30

"Perchance to Dream" (Franzen), 2, 3, 4, 5, 20

performing arts, 106, 132–34, 143, 144, 163

personal ambition, novels about, 17–18, 62–63

Pirke Aboth (Ethics of the Fathers), 85–89

Plato, *The Republic,* 131, 132–34, 143

Platonic theory of art, 131–34

pleasure, 157–60, 165

pluralism, 70, 160

Podhoretz, Norman, 8, 154

"Poet as Hero: Keats in His Letters, The" (Trilling), 146–50

poetry: Arnold's turn from, 49–50, 53; cultural decline of, 2, 3; familiar conventions of, 13; Ginsberg and, 112, 113, 115, 118–21, 124–27; Keats and, 149; literary critics and, 20, 51; Plato's case against, 132–33; Wordsworth and, 87–88, 121–24

pogroms, 82

politics, 7–8, 153–55; neoconservatives and, 8, 42, 62; student protests (1968) and, 153–54. *See also* conservatism; liberalism

Popular Front, 42, 65, 153; Trilling critique of, 42–43, 44, 59

"Portrait of the Artist as an American" (Trilling), 45–47

postmodernism, 17, 18

power. modernist writers on, 89

primal truth, 111–12

Princess Casamassima, The (James), 64–69, 70

proletarian novels, 52

Proust, Marcel, 31, 45, 54, 75, 94, 95, 98; *Cities of the Plain,* 31; *Remembrance of Things Past,* 95

Public Interest (magazine), 42

rabbinic sages, 85–89

radicalism, 64–65, 66–67, 69

Rahv, Philip, 78

Rameau, Jean-Philippe, 102, 103

Rameau's Nephew (Diderot), 101–4, 107, 133–34, 144, 150, 152

Rand, Ayn, *The Fountainhead,* 89

reading: author's will and, 5, 109; connectedness of, 14–17, 20, 97–98, 157–58; consensus about important works and, 97; decline in, 3; naïve approach and, 131, 146; as novelistic device, 27–28; pleasure from, 157; self-creation through, 22, 167–68

realism, 17–20, 52; Manifesto (1932) on, 45; social problem novels and., 42–47, 52, 57, 65; Trilling essays on, 46–47. *See also* moral realism

reality: mind and, 66–67, 123, 124, 125; Trilling essay on, 12, 19, 35,

Dean Howells and the Roots of Modern Taste," 135–37; "Wordsworth and the Rabbis," 78, 84–89, 111–12; Fiction: *The Journey Abandoned* (unfinished novel), 6–7, 25, 31–32; *The Middle of the Journey,* 6, 24, 25–29, 59, 65, 121; "Of This Time, Of That Place," 125–27; "The Other Margaret," 65

Truman, Harry, 40

truth, 68–69, 111–12, 148

"T. S. Eliot's Politics" (Trilling), 43–44

Twain, Mark, 96

Updike, John, 2

utopianism: liberal renunciation of, 70; Morris novel on, 155–57, 165

Valéry, Paul, 95

values, 43, 52, 134–50, 167–68

Van Doren, Mark, 30

visual arts, 163

Voltaire, 63

Warshow, Robert, 25–26

Warwick, Dionne, 160

"we" rhetorical device, 11–13, 84–85, 97

West, Cornel, 8

Whitman, Walt, 151–52, 164; *Democratic Vistas,* 151–52

"Why We Read Jane Austen" (Trilling), 137

wickedness, 33–34

Wieseltier, Leon, 6

will: as Trilling key word, 11. *See also* artistic will

"William Dean Howells and the Roots of Modern Taste" (Trilling), 135–37

Wilson, Edmund, 9, 14, 21, 45; *Axel's Castle,* 95; Trilling's critical approach vs., 21, 95, 96

Wolfe, Tom, 17–18, 19, 66; "Stalking the Billion-Footed Beast," 17–18

Wordsworth, William, 111–12, 121–24; "Intimations of Immortality," 121–24; "The Prelude," 87–88, 124; "Tintern Abbey," 124; Trilling essays on, 78, 84–89, 111–12, 121–24, 125

"Wordsworth and the Rabbis" (Trilling), 78, 84–89, 111–12

working-class portrayals, 64–65, 66–67

Yeats, William Butler, 45, 89, 94, 95, 98; on aging, 121; "Meru," 152

Zionism, 82

Adam Kirsch is a senior editor at the *New Republic* and a columnist for *Tablet* magazine. Formerly the book critic for the *New York Sun* newspaper, his essays and reviews have appeared in many publications, including the *New Yorker,* the *New York Review of Books,* and the *TLS.* He is the author of two books of poems, *The Thousand Wells* and *Invasions,* and two books of criticism, *The Wounded Surgeon: Confession and Transformation in Six American Poets* and *The Modern Element: Essays on Contemporary Poetry.* His most recent book is a short biography, *Benjamin Disraeli.*